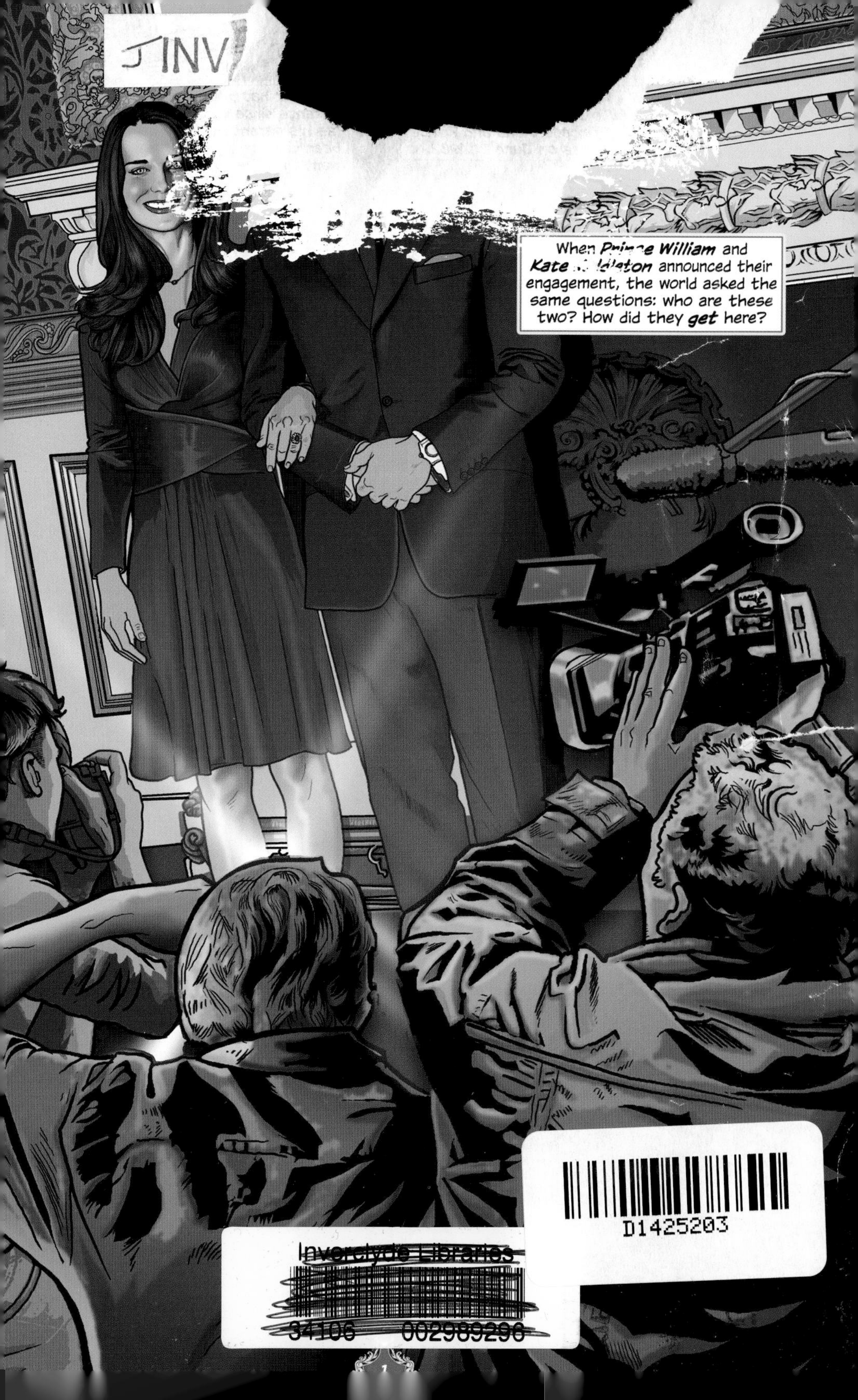
When Prince William and Kate Middleton announced their engagement, the world asked the same questions: who are these two? How did they get here?

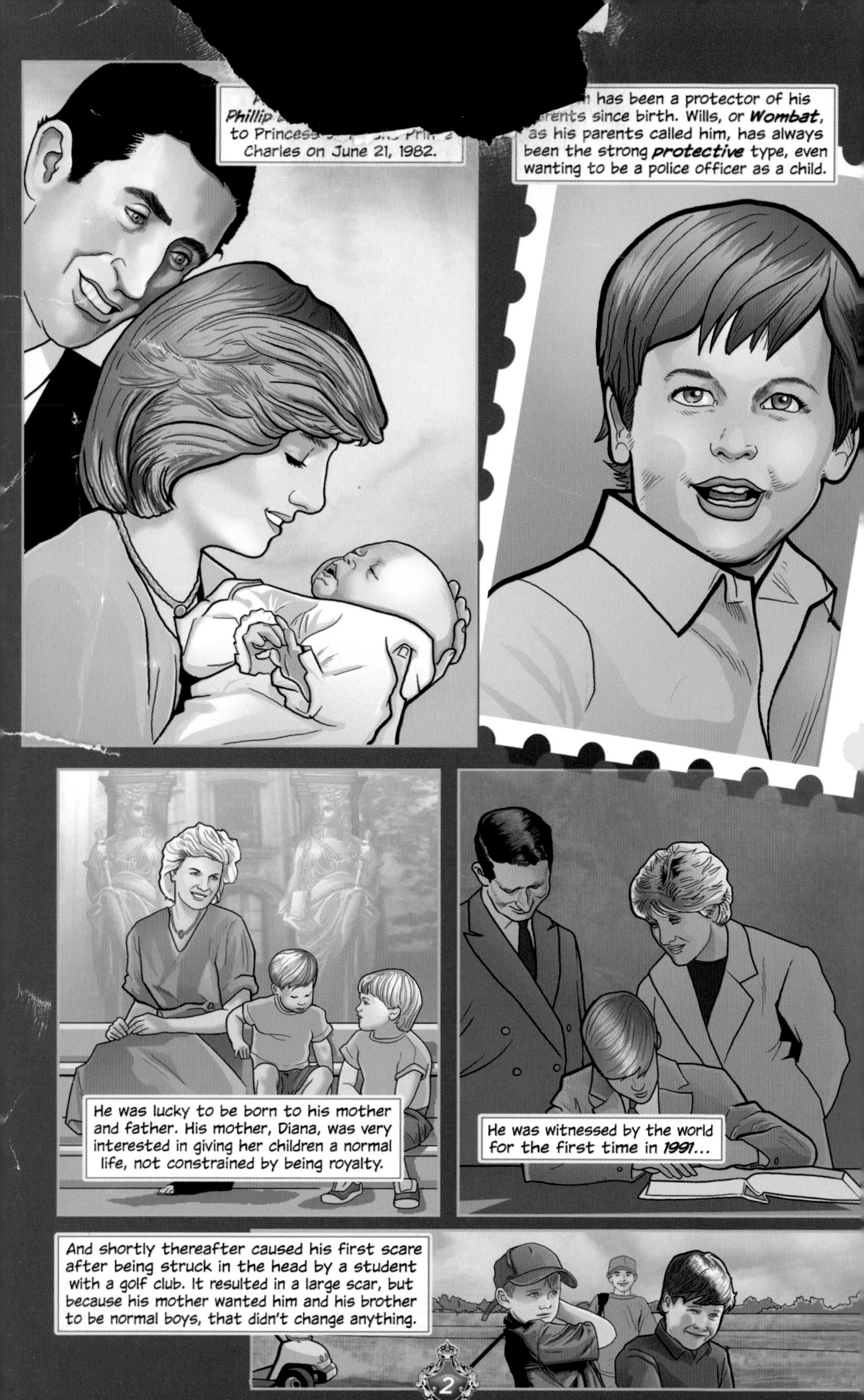
[redacted] Phillip [redacted] to Princess [redacted] Charles on June 21, 1982.
[redacted] has been a protector of his [redacted] since birth. Wills, or Wombat, as his parents called him, has always been the strong protective type, even wanting to be a police officer as a child.
He was lucky to be born to his mother and father. His mother, Diana, was very interested in giving her children a normal life, not constrained by being royalty.
He was witnessed by the world for the first time in 1991...
And shortly thereafter caused his first scare after being struck in the head by a student with a golf club. It resulted in a large scar, but because his mother wanted him and his brother to be normal boys, that didn't change anything.

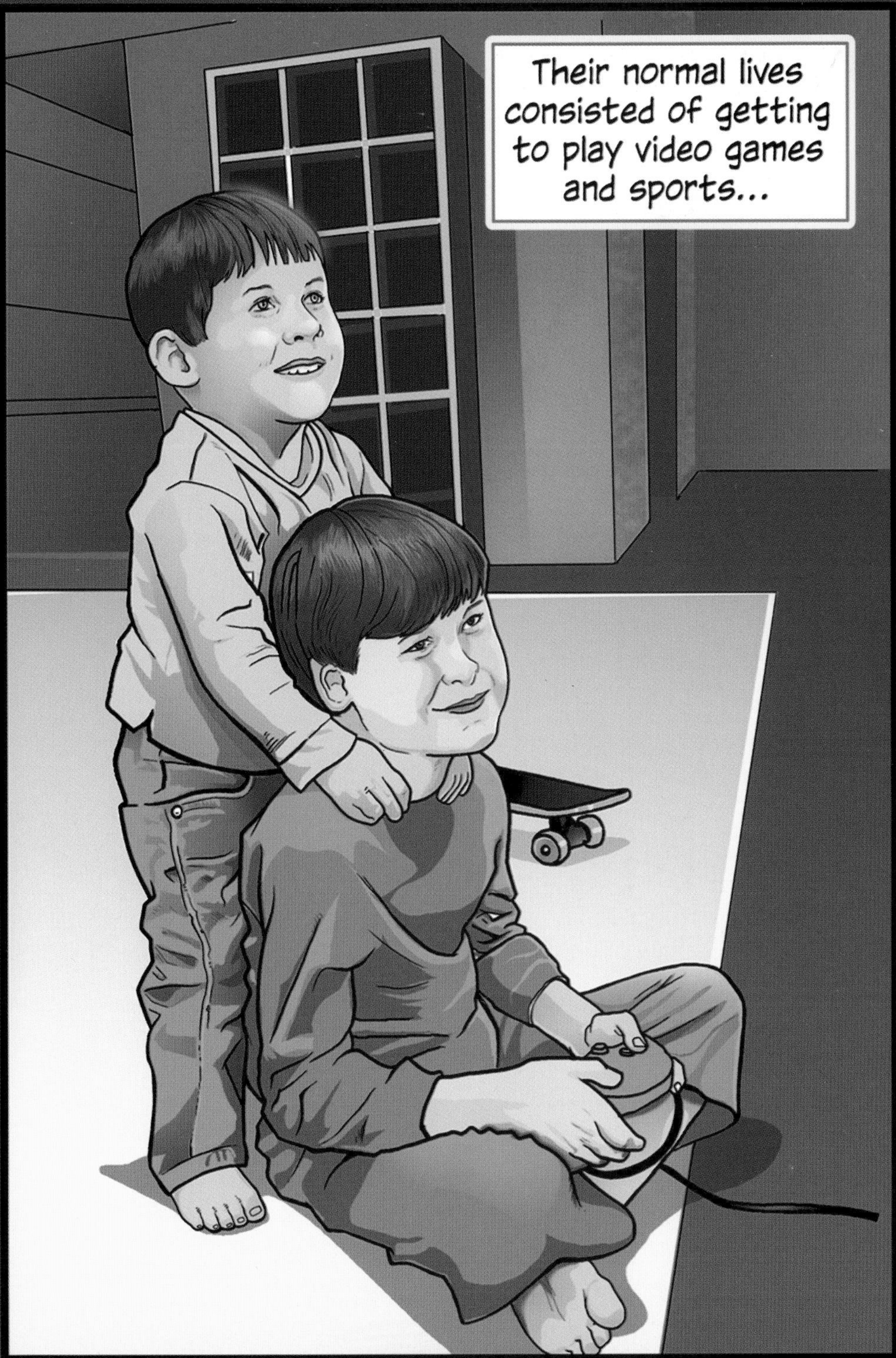
Their normal lives consisted of getting to play video games and sports...

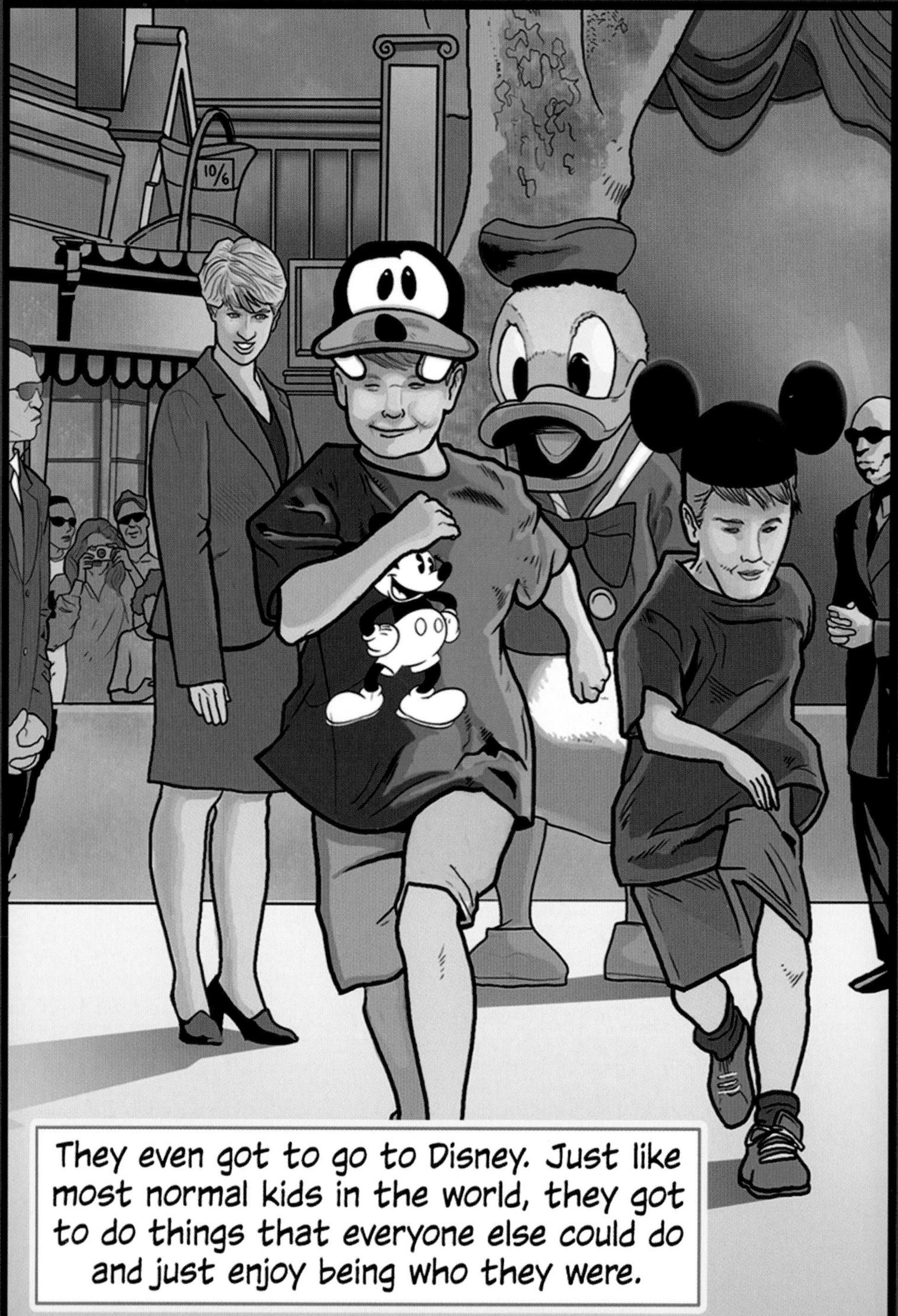
10/6
They even got to go to Disney. Just like most normal kids in the world, they got to do things that everyone else could do and just enjoy being who they were.

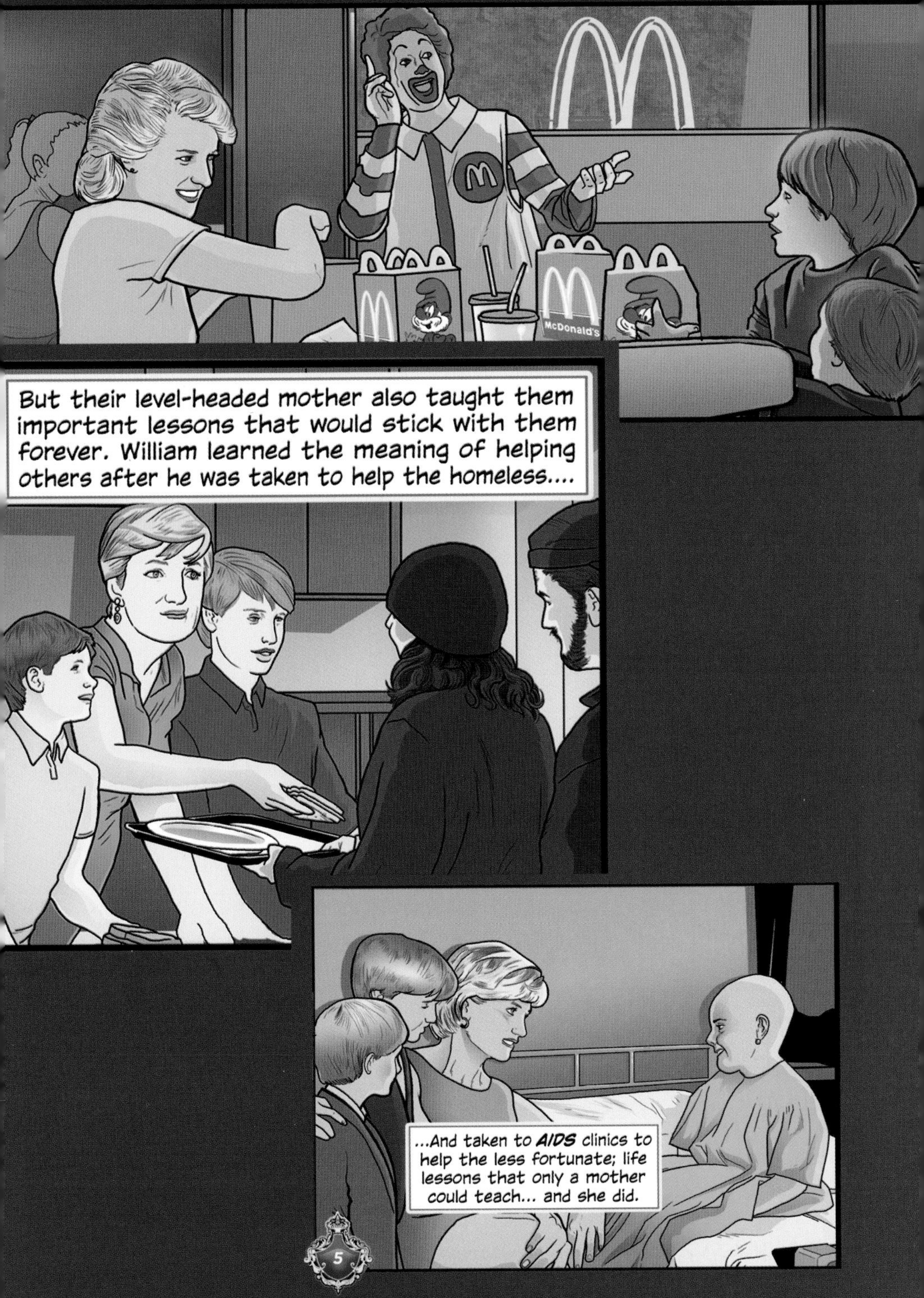
McDonald's
But their level-headed mother also taught them important lessons that would stick with them forever. William learned the meaning of helping others after he was taken to help the homeless....
...And taken to AIDS clinics to help the less fortunate; life lessons that only a mother could teach... and she did.

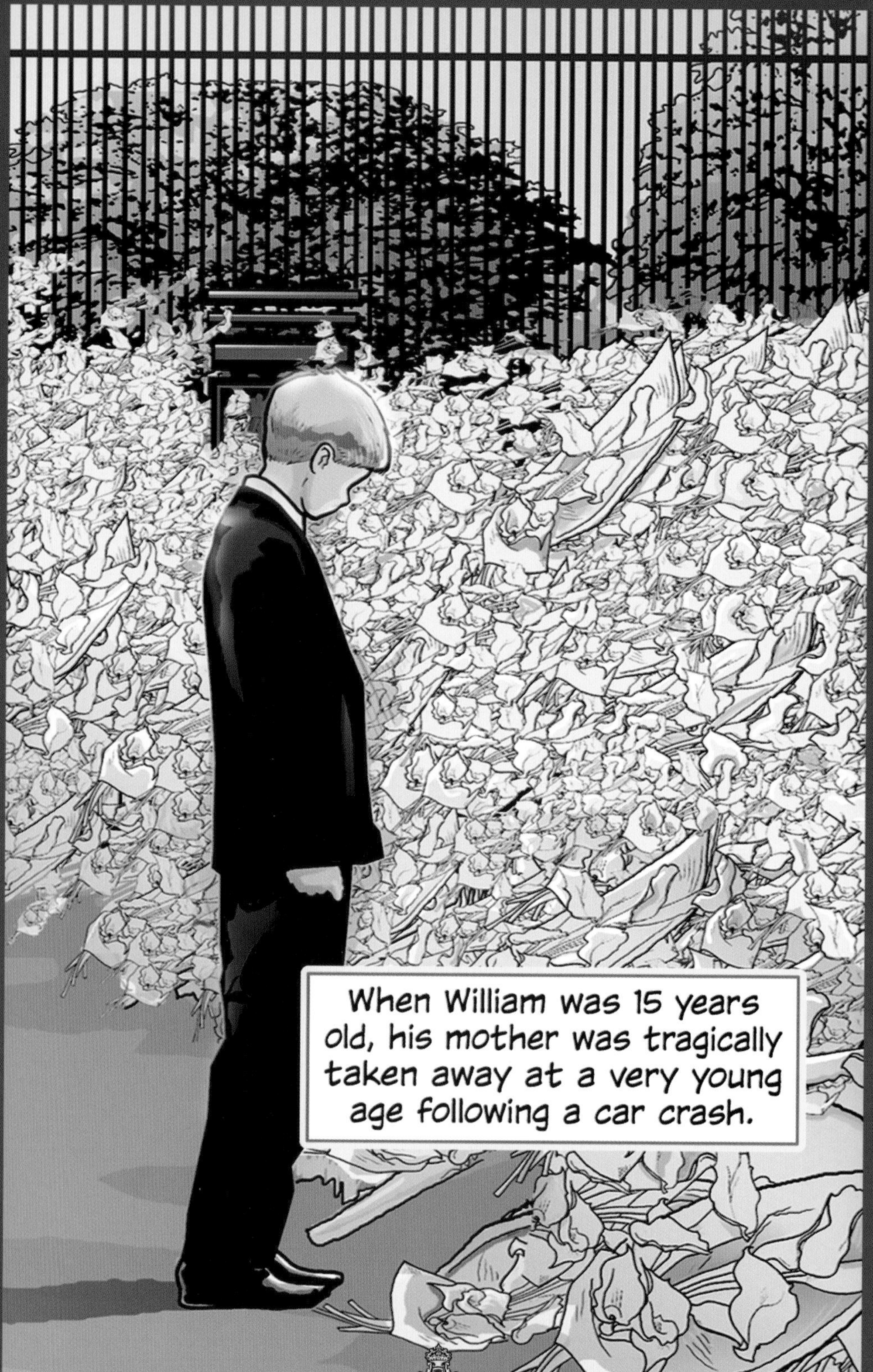
When William was 15 years old, his mother was tragically taken away at a very young age following a car crash.

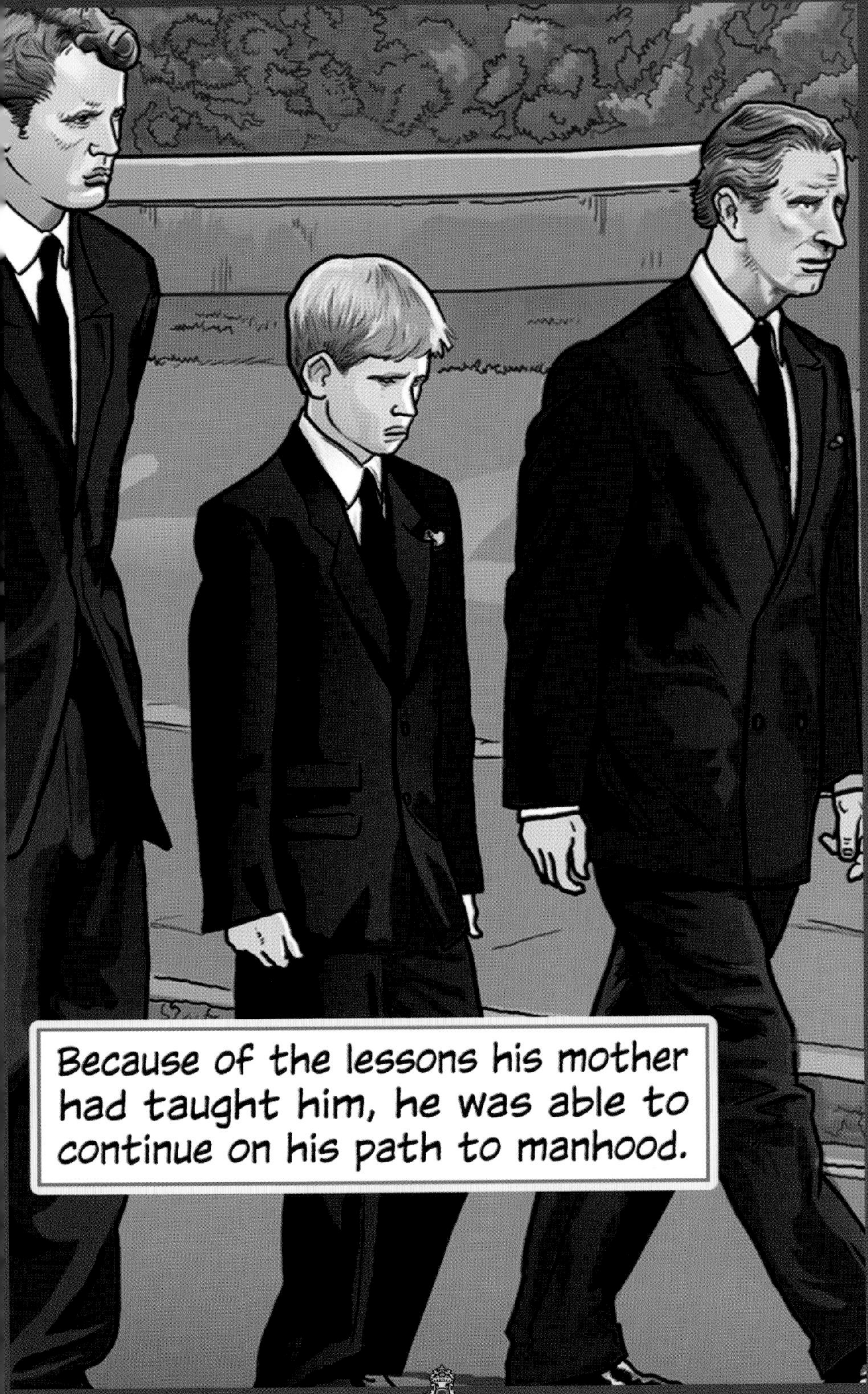
Because of the lessons his mother had taught him, he was able to continue on his path to manhood.

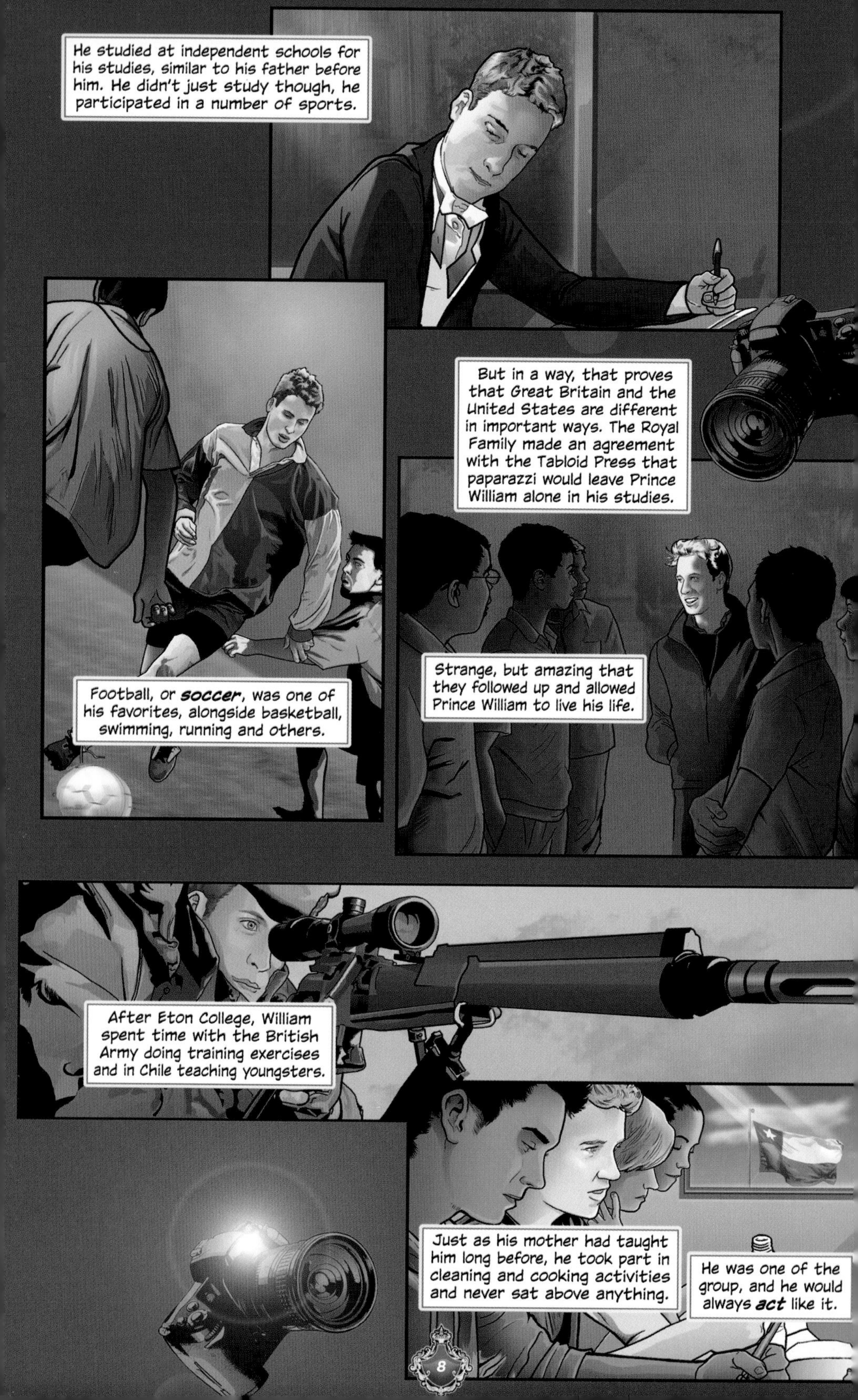
He studied at independent schools for his studies, similar to his father before him. He didn't just study though, he participated in a number of sports.
Football, or **soccer**, was one of his favorites, alongside basketball, swimming, running and others.
But in a way, that proves that Great Britain and the United States are different in important ways. The Royal Family made an agreement with the Tabloid Press that paparazzi would leave Prince William alone in his studies.
Strange, but amazing that they followed up and allowed Prince William to live his life.
After Eton College, William spent time with the British Army doing training exercises and in Chile teaching youngsters.
Just as his mother had taught him long before, he took part in cleaning and cooking activities and never sat above anything.
He was one of the group, and he would always **act** like it.
8

William applied and was enrolled the University of St. Andrews in 2001 under the name William Wales. didn't matter. Wherever he went, attention managed to follow him.

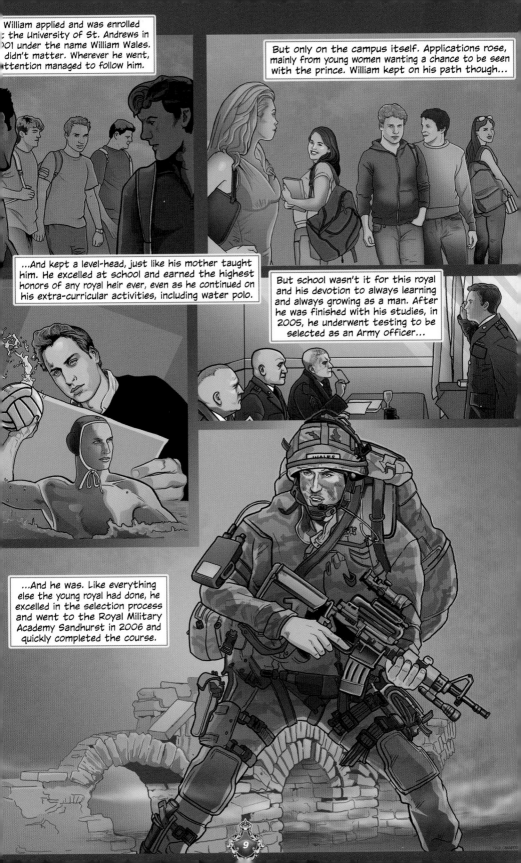

But only on the campus itself. Applications rose, mainly from young women wanting a chance to be seen with the prince. William kept on his path though...

...And kept a level-head, just like his mother taught him. He excelled at school and earned the highest honors of any royal heir ever, even as he continued on his extra-curricular activities, including water polo.

But school wasn't it for this royal and his devotion to always learning and always growing as a man. After he was finished with his studies, in 2005, he underwent testing to be selected as an Army officer...

...And he was. Like everything else the young royal had done, he excelled in the selection process and went to the Royal Military Academy Sandhurst in 2006 and quickly completed the course.

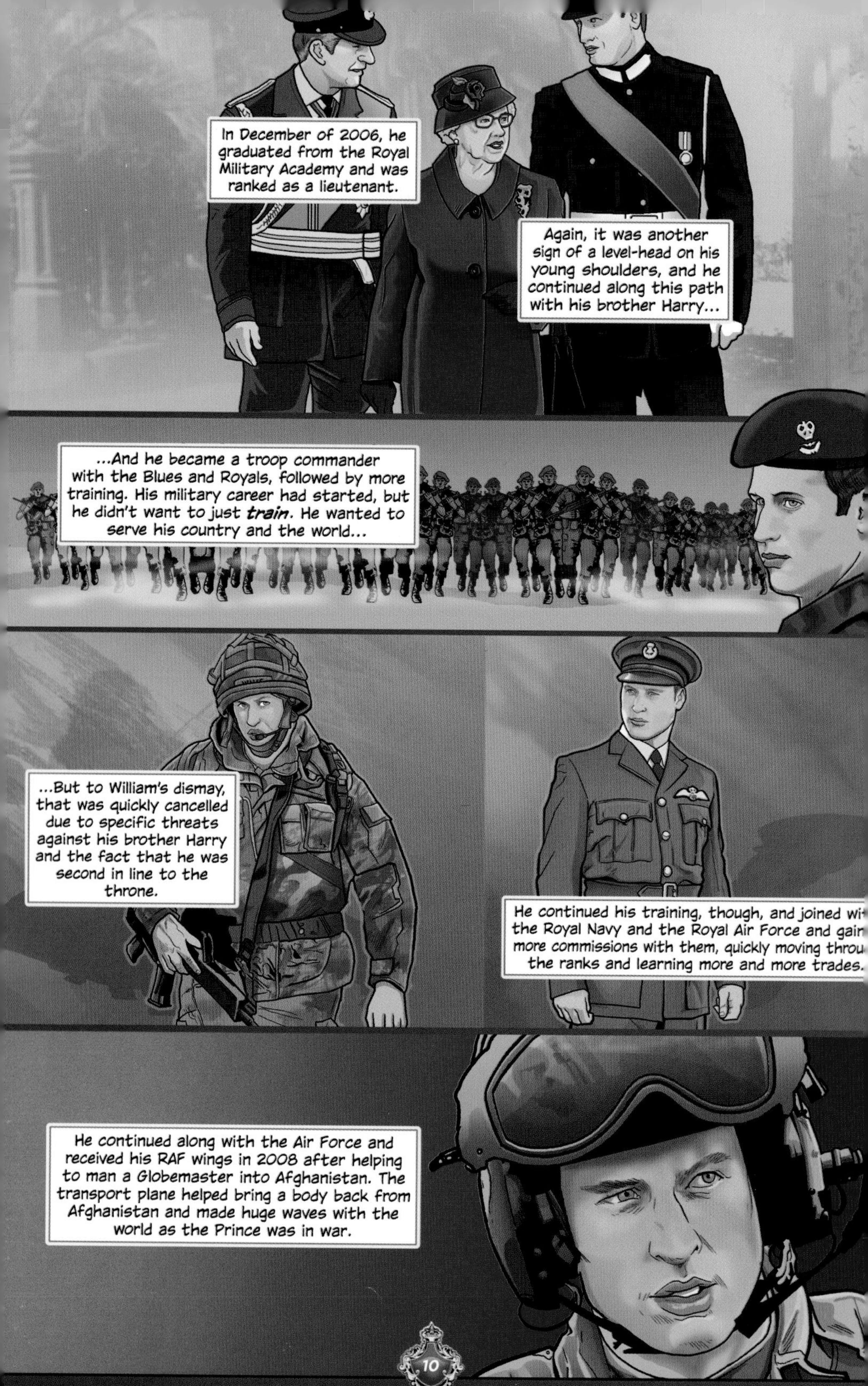
In December of 2006, he graduated from the Royal Military Academy and was ranked as a lieutenant.
Again, it was another sign of a level-head on his young shoulders, and he continued along this path with his brother Harry...
...And he became a troop commander with the Blues and Royals, followed by more training. His military career had started, but he didn't want to just *train*. He wanted to serve his country and the world...
...But to William's dismay, that was quickly cancelled due to specific threats against his brother Harry and the fact that he was second in line to the throne.
He continued his training, though, and joined wi the Royal Navy and the Royal Air Force and gair more commissions with them, quickly moving throu the ranks and learning more and more trades.
He continued along with the Air Force and received his RAF wings in 2008 after helping to man a Globemaster into Afghanistan. The transport plane helped bring a body back from Afghanistan and made huge waves with the world as the Prince was in war.

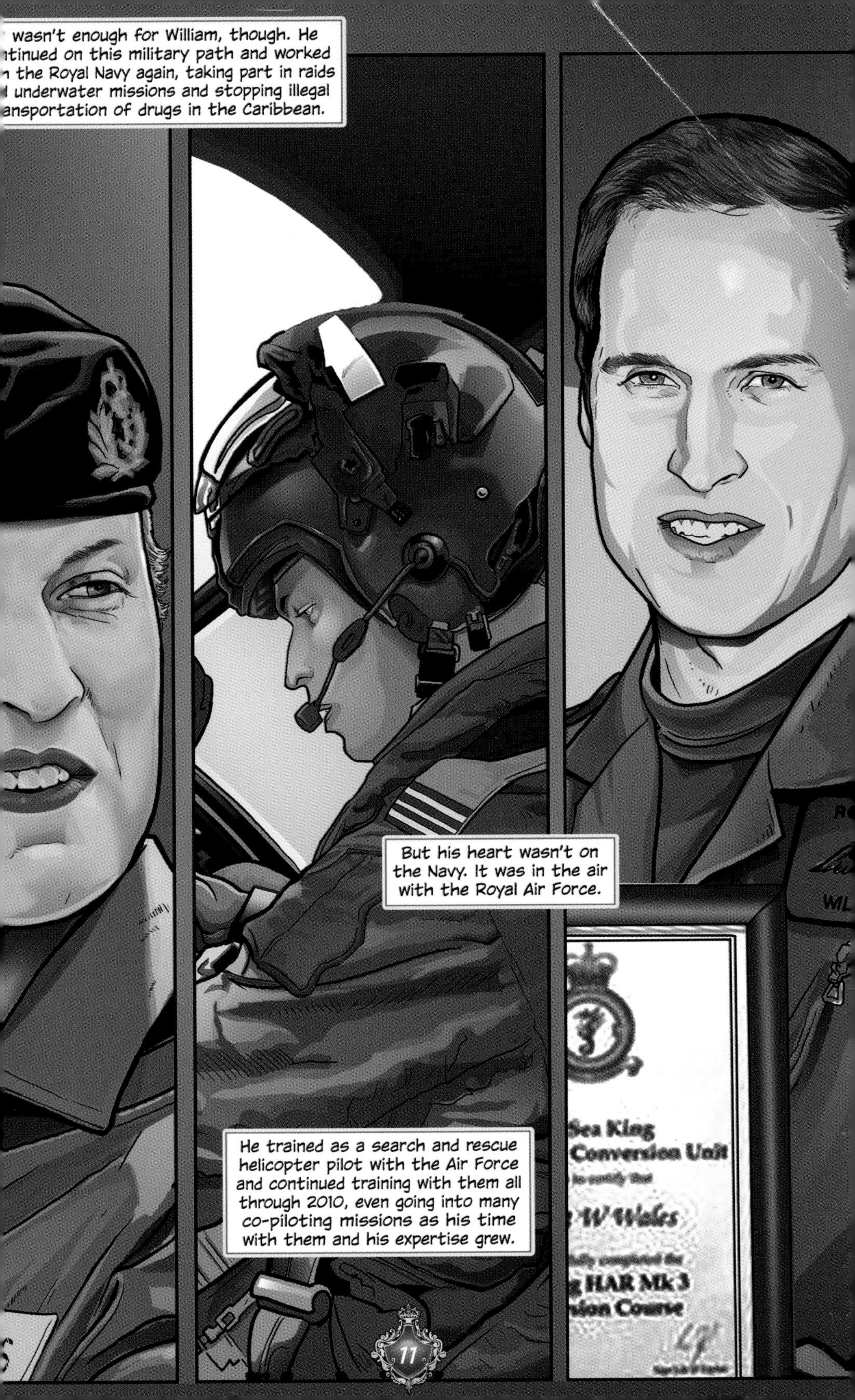

wasn't enough for William, though. He
tinued on this military path and worked
the Royal Navy again, taking part in raids
underwater missions and stopping illegal
ansportation of drugs in the Caribbean.
But his heart wasn't on the Navy. It was in the air with the Royal Air Force.
He trained as a search and rescue helicopter pilot with the Air Force and continued training with them all through 2010, even going into many co-piloting missions as his time with them and his expertise grew.
Sea King
Conversion Unit
W Wales
HAR Mk 3
sion Course

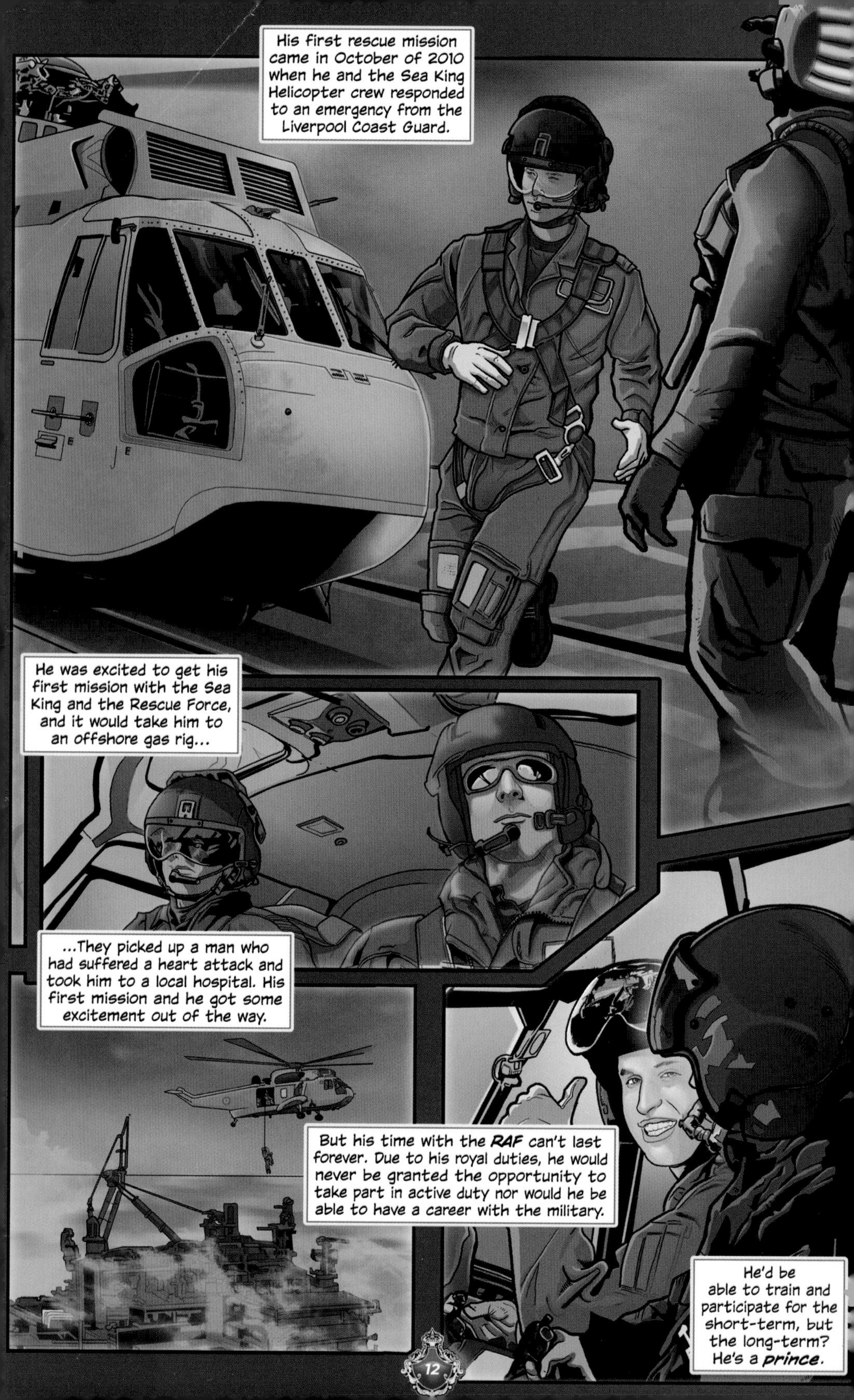

His first rescue mission came in October of 2010 when he and the Sea King Helicopter crew responded to an emergency from the Liverpool Coast Guard.
He was excited to get his first mission with the Sea King and the Rescue Force, and it would take him to an offshore gas rig...
...They picked up a man who had suffered a heart attack and took him to a local hospital. His first mission and he got some excitement out of the way.
But his time with the RAF can't last forever. Due to his royal duties, he would never be granted the opportunity to take part in active duty nor would he be able to have a career with the military.
He'd be able to train and participate for the short-term, but the long-term? He's a prince.

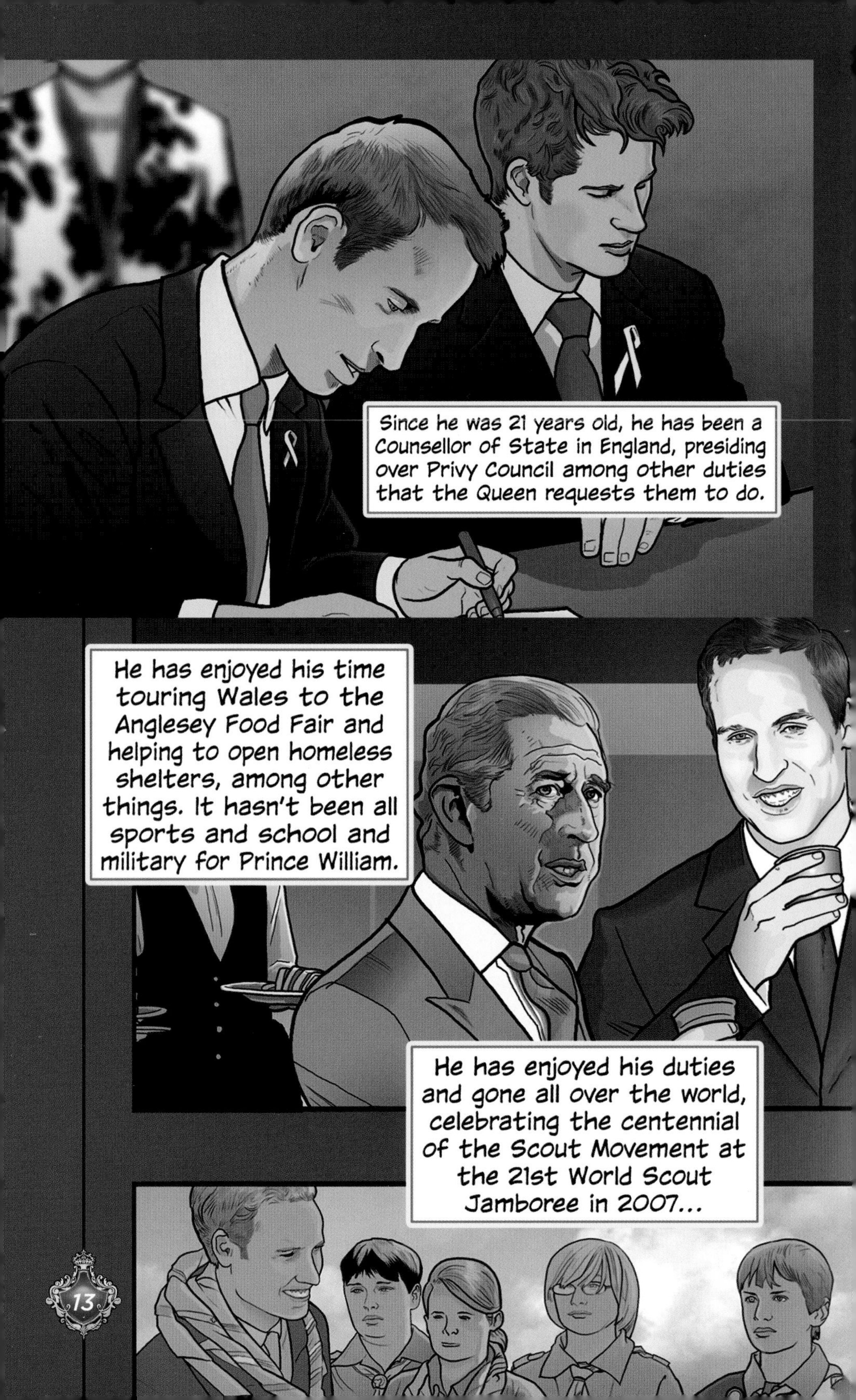
Since he was 21 years old, he has been a Counsellor of State in England, presiding over Privy Council among other duties that the Queen requests them to do.
He has enjoyed his time touring Wales to the Anglesey Food Fair and helping to open homeless shelters, among other things. It hasn't been all sports and school and military for Prince William.
He has enjoyed his duties and gone all over the world, celebrating the centennial of the Scout Movement at the 21st World Scout Jamboree in 2007...

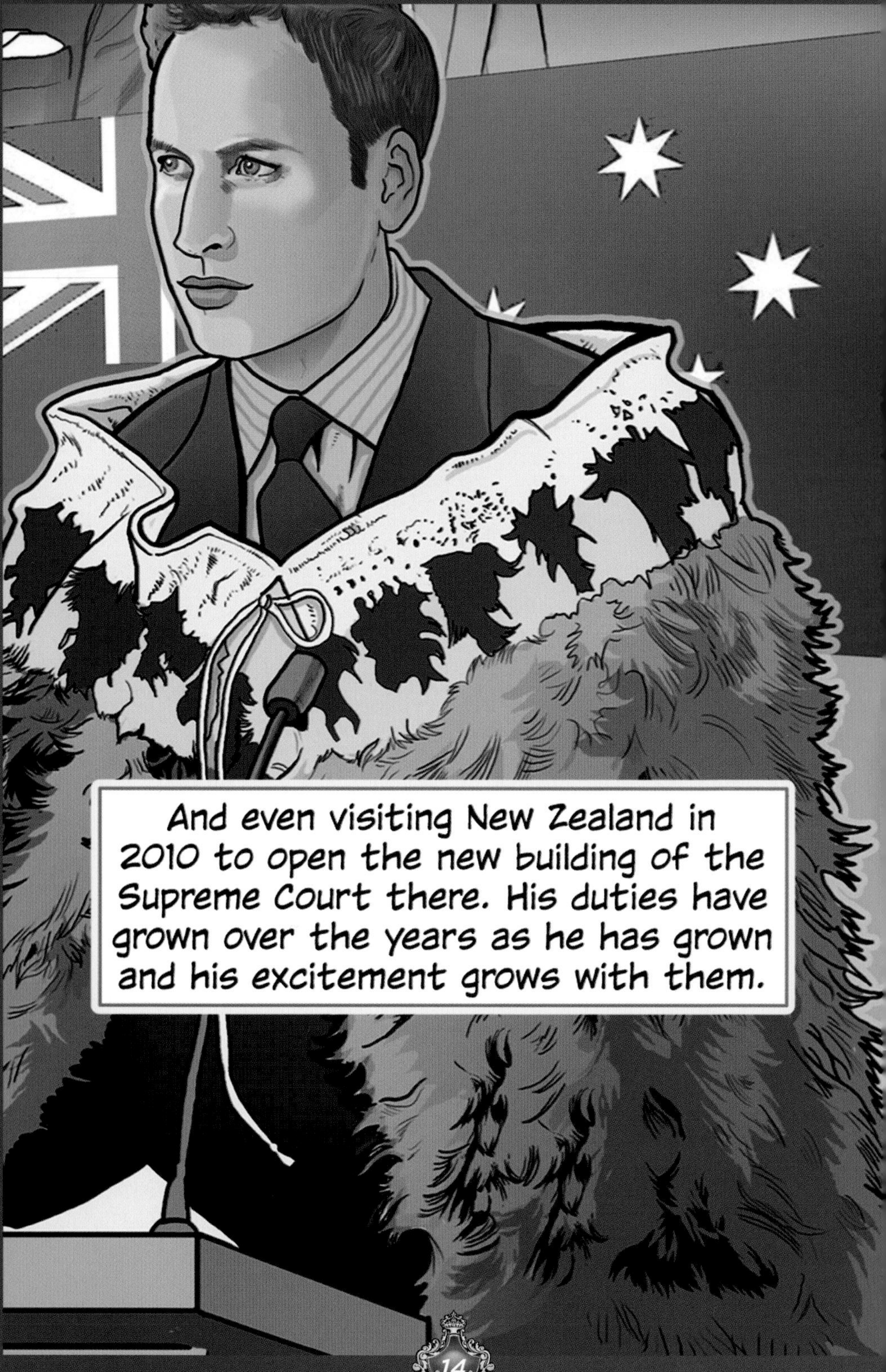
And even visiting New Zealand in 2010 to open the new building of the Supreme Court there. His duties have grown over the years as he has grown and his excitement grows with them.

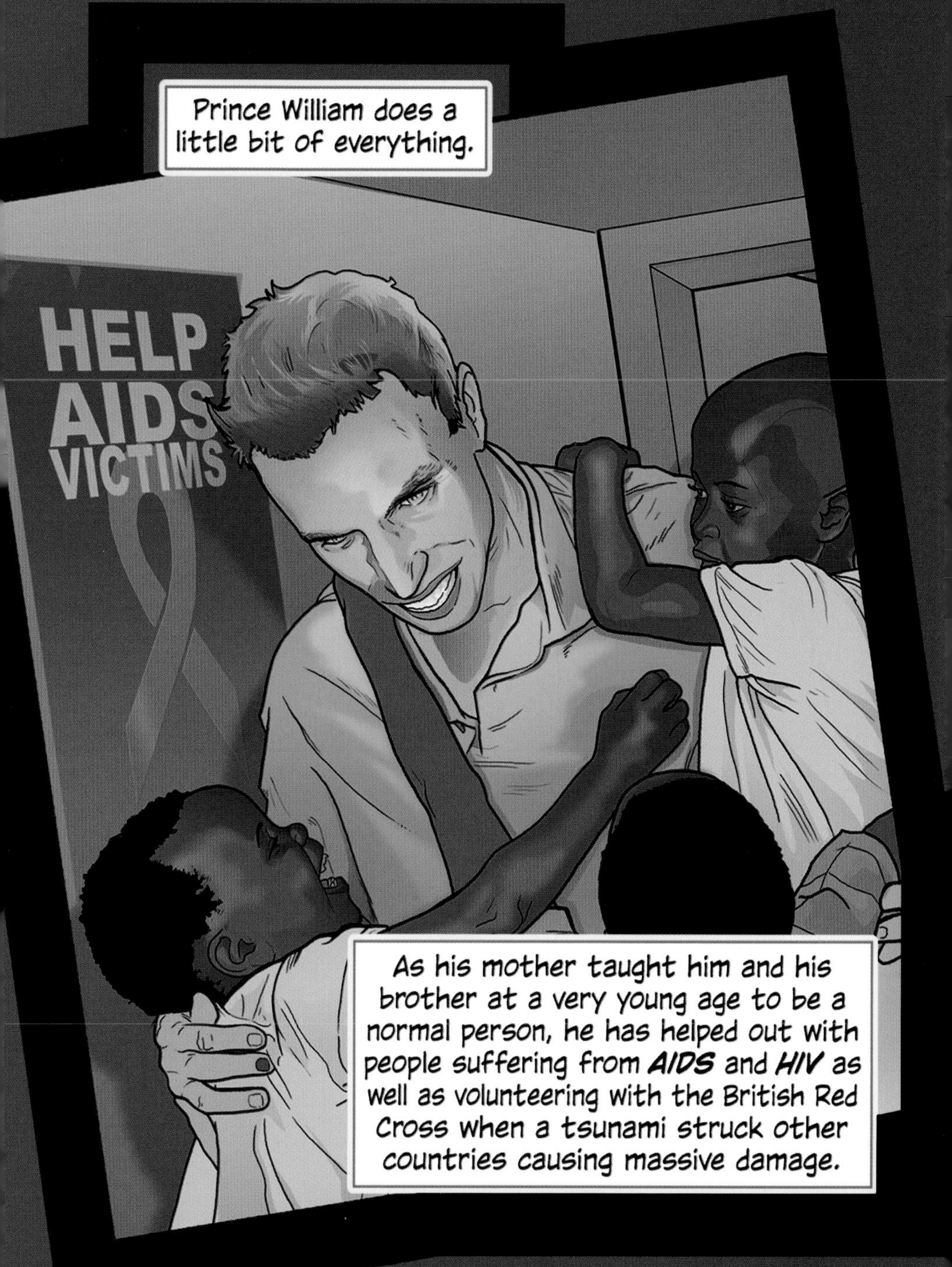
Prince William does a little bit of everything.
HELP AIDS VICTIMS
As his mother taught him and his brother at a very young age to be a normal person, he has helped out with people suffering from ***AIDS*** and ***HIV*** as well as volunteering with the British Red Cross when a tsunami struck other countries causing massive damage.

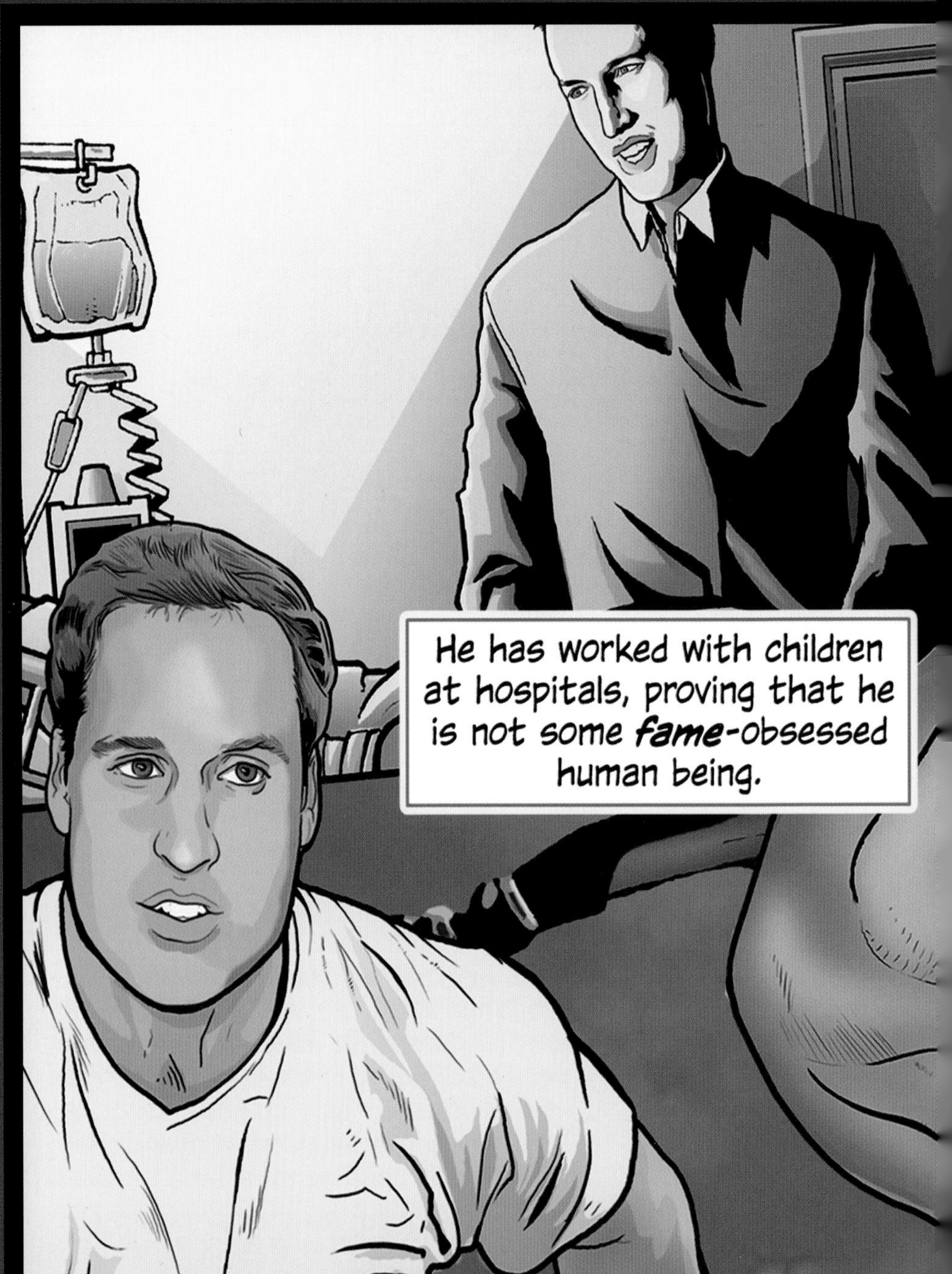
He has worked with children at hospitals, proving that he is not some *fame*-obsessed human being.

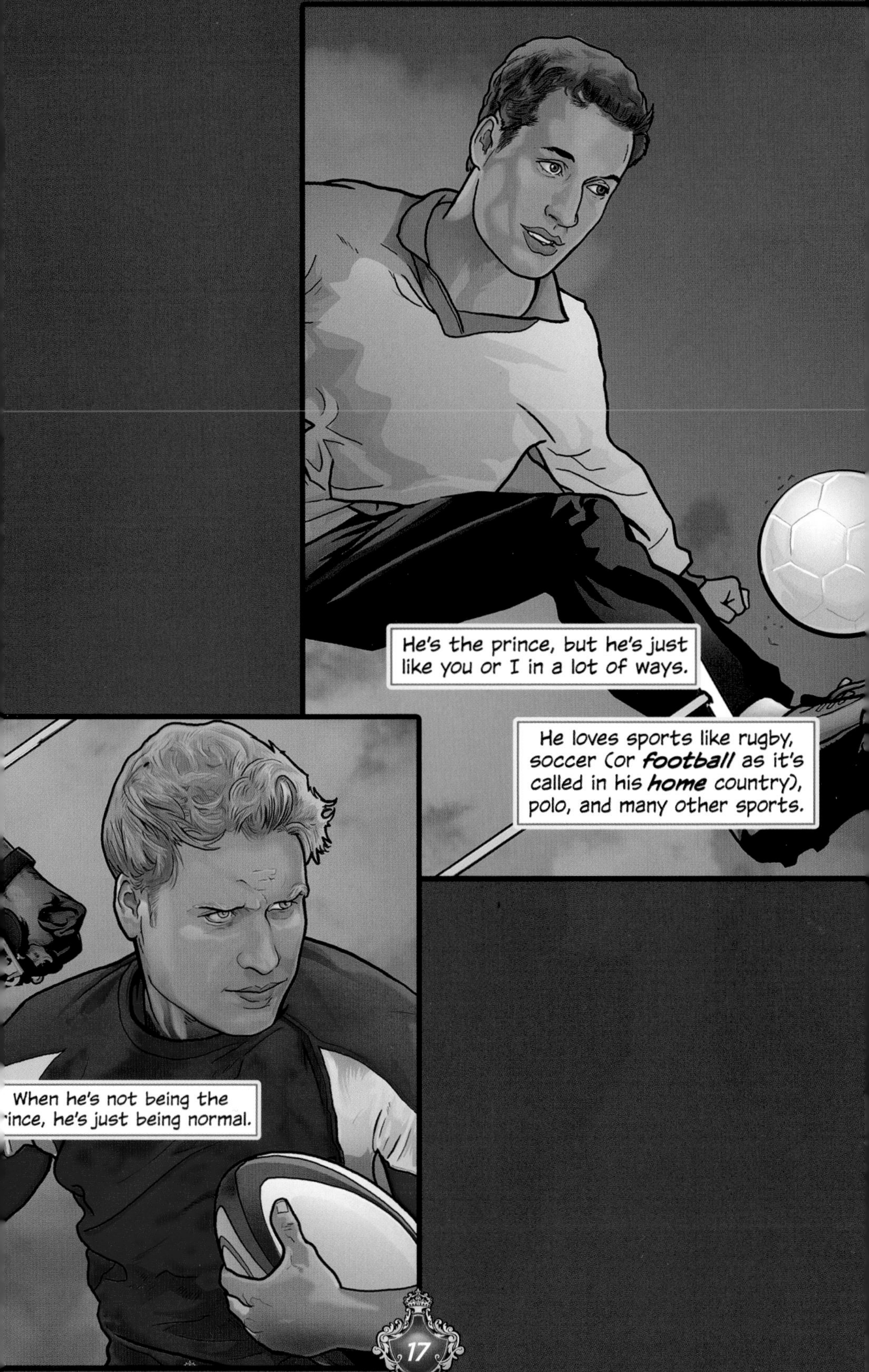
He's the prince, but he's just like you or I in a lot of ways.
He loves sports like rugby, soccer (or ***football*** as it's called in his ***home*** country), polo, and many other sports.
When he's not being the rince, he's just being normal.

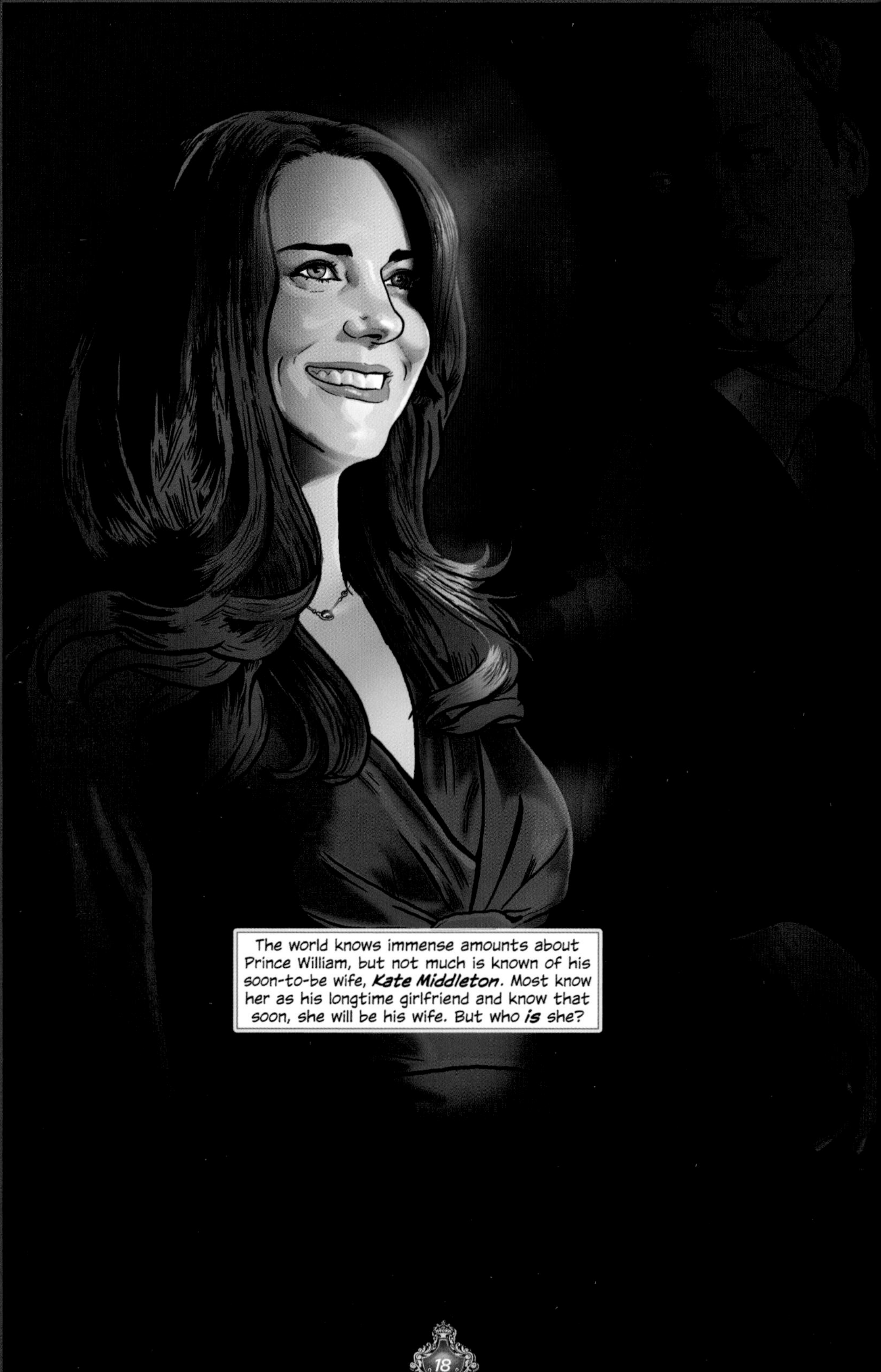
The world knows immense amounts about Prince William, but not much is known of his soon-to-be wife, *Kate Middleton*. Most know her as his longtime girlfriend and know that soon, she will be his wife. But who *is* she?

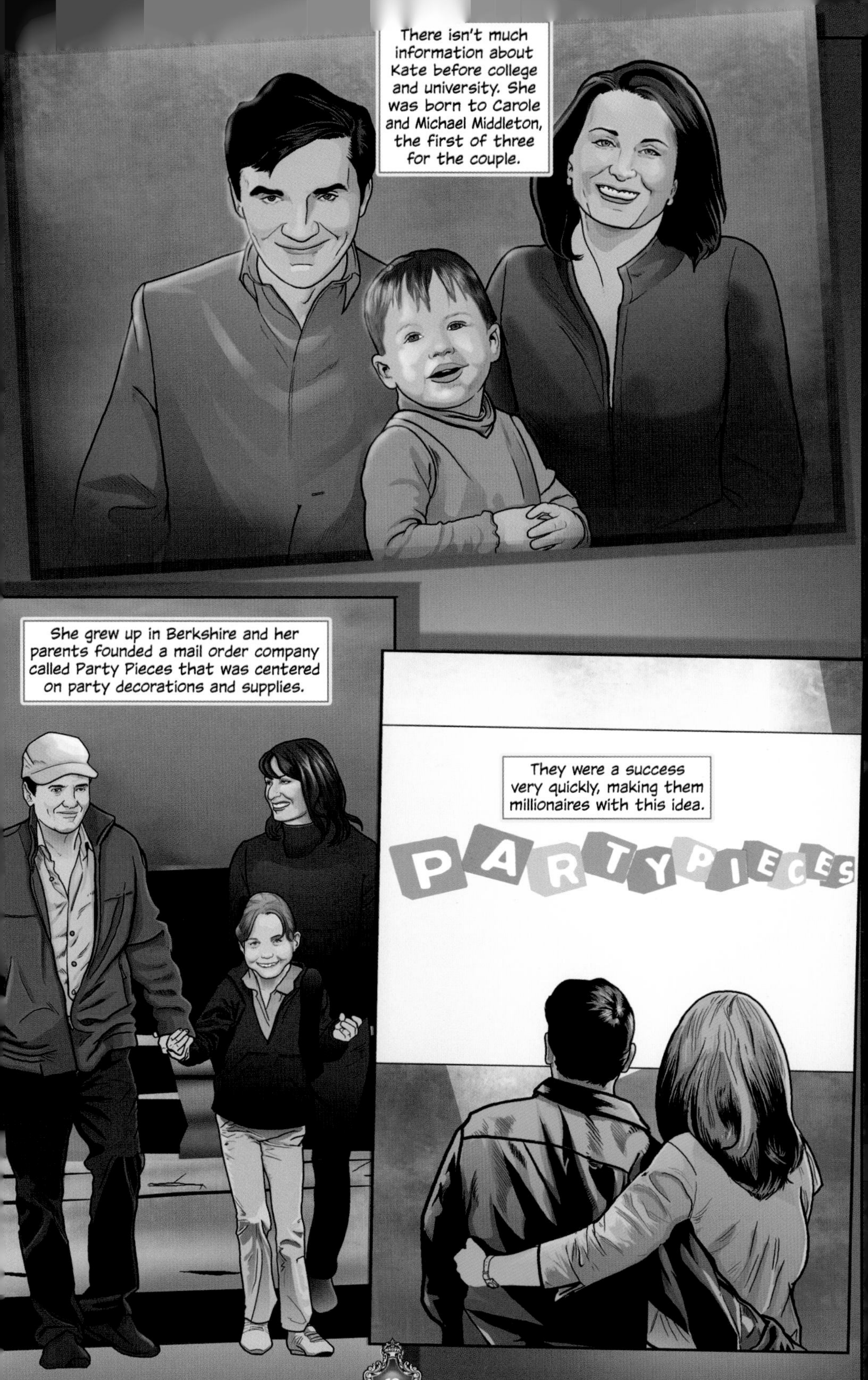
There isn't much information about Kate before college and university. She was born to Carole and Michael Middleton, the first of three for the couple.
She grew up in Berkshire and her parents founded a mail order company called Party Pieces that was centered on party decorations and supplies.
They were a success very quickly, making them millionaires with this idea.
PARTYPIECES

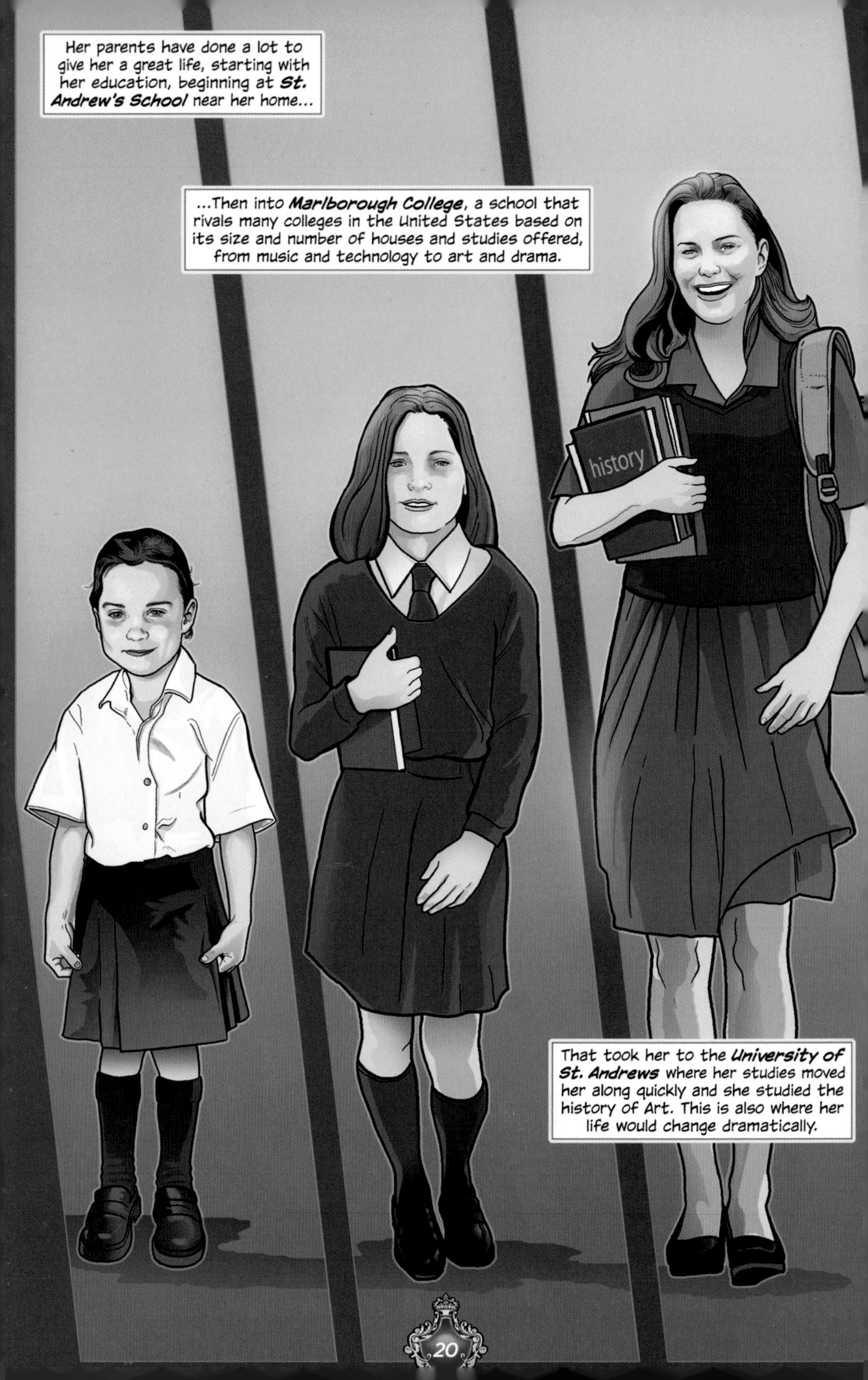
Her parents have done a lot to give her a great life, starting with her education, beginning at St. Andrew's School near her home...
...Then into Marlborough College, a school that rivals many colleges in the United States based on its size and number of houses and studies offered, from music and technology to art and drama.
history
That took her to the University of St. Andrews where her studies moved her along quickly and she studied the history of Art. This is also where her life would change dramatically.

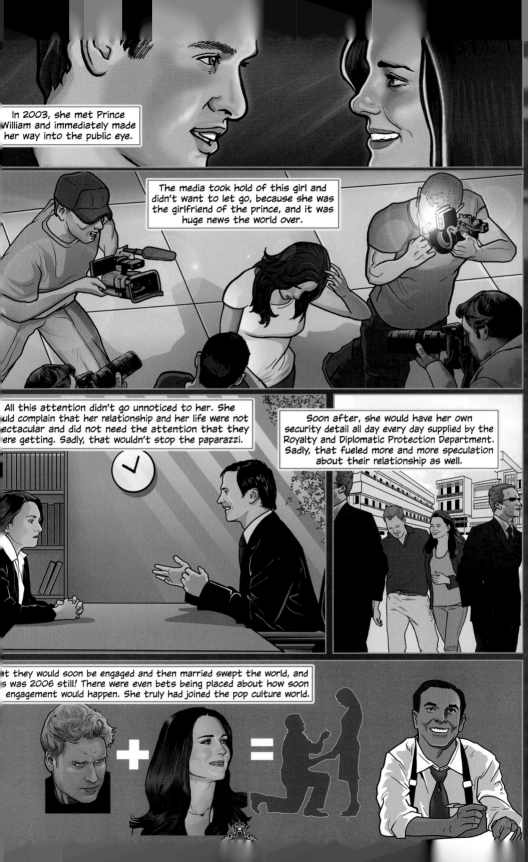

In 2003, she met Prince William and immediately made her way into the public eye.

The media took hold of this girl and didn't want to let go, because she was the girlfriend of the prince, and it was huge news the world over.

All this attention didn't go unnoticed to her. She would complain that her relationship and her life were not spectacular and did not need the attention that they were getting. Sadly, that wouldn't stop the paparazzi.

Soon after, she would have her own security detail all day every day supplied by the Royalty and Diplomatic Protection Department. Sadly, that fueled more and more speculation about their relationship as well.

that they would soon be engaged and then married swept the world, and this was 2006 still! There were even bets being placed about how soon the engagement would happen. She truly had joined the pop culture world.

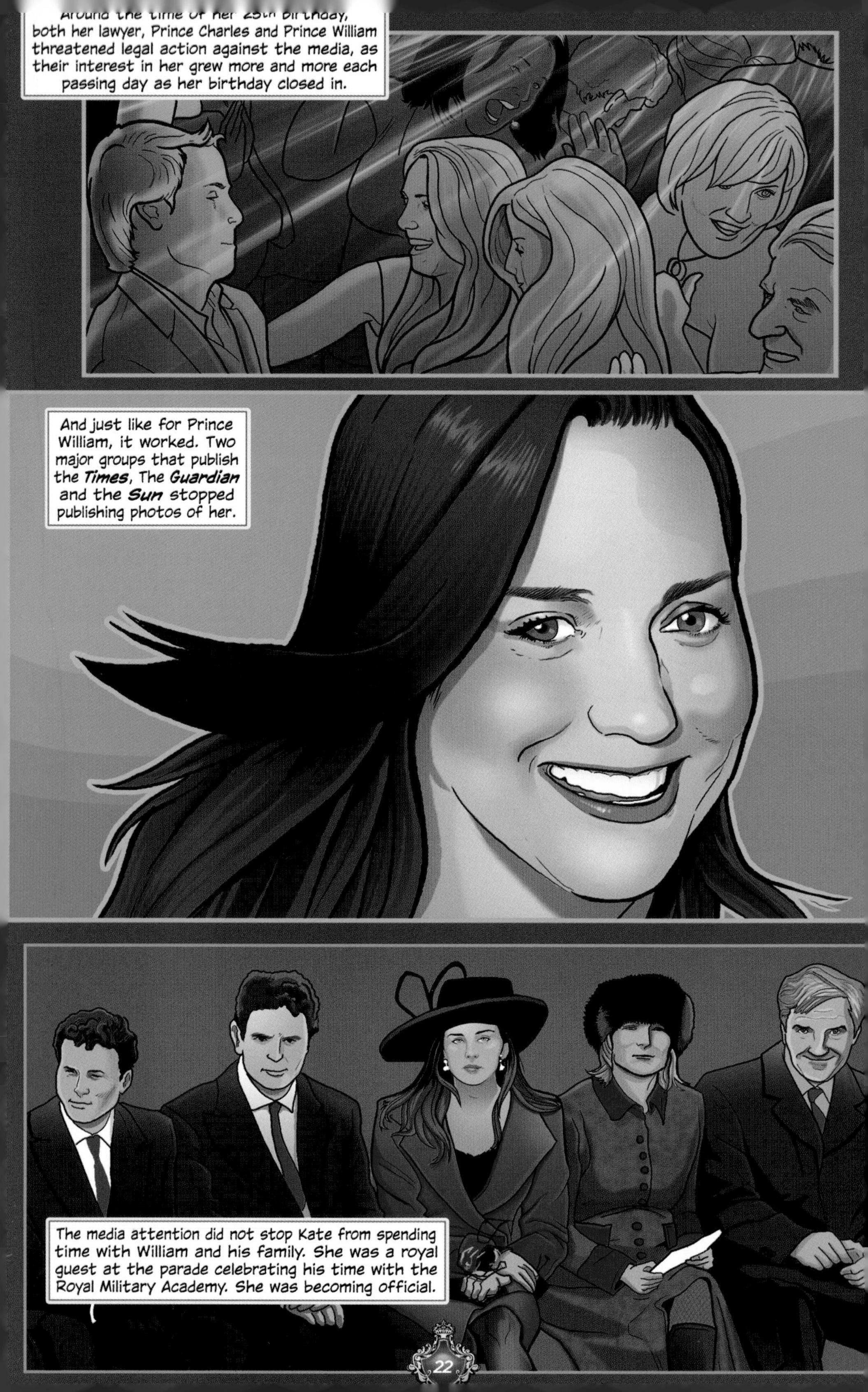

Around the time of her 25th birthday, both her lawyer, Prince Charles and Prince William threatened legal action against the media, as their interest in her grew more and more each passing day as her birthday closed in.
And just like for Prince William, it worked. Two major groups that publish the *Times*, The *Guardian* and the *Sun* stopped publishing photos of her.
The media attention did not stop Kate from spending time with William and his family. She was a royal guest at the parade celebrating his time with the Royal Military Academy. She was becoming official.

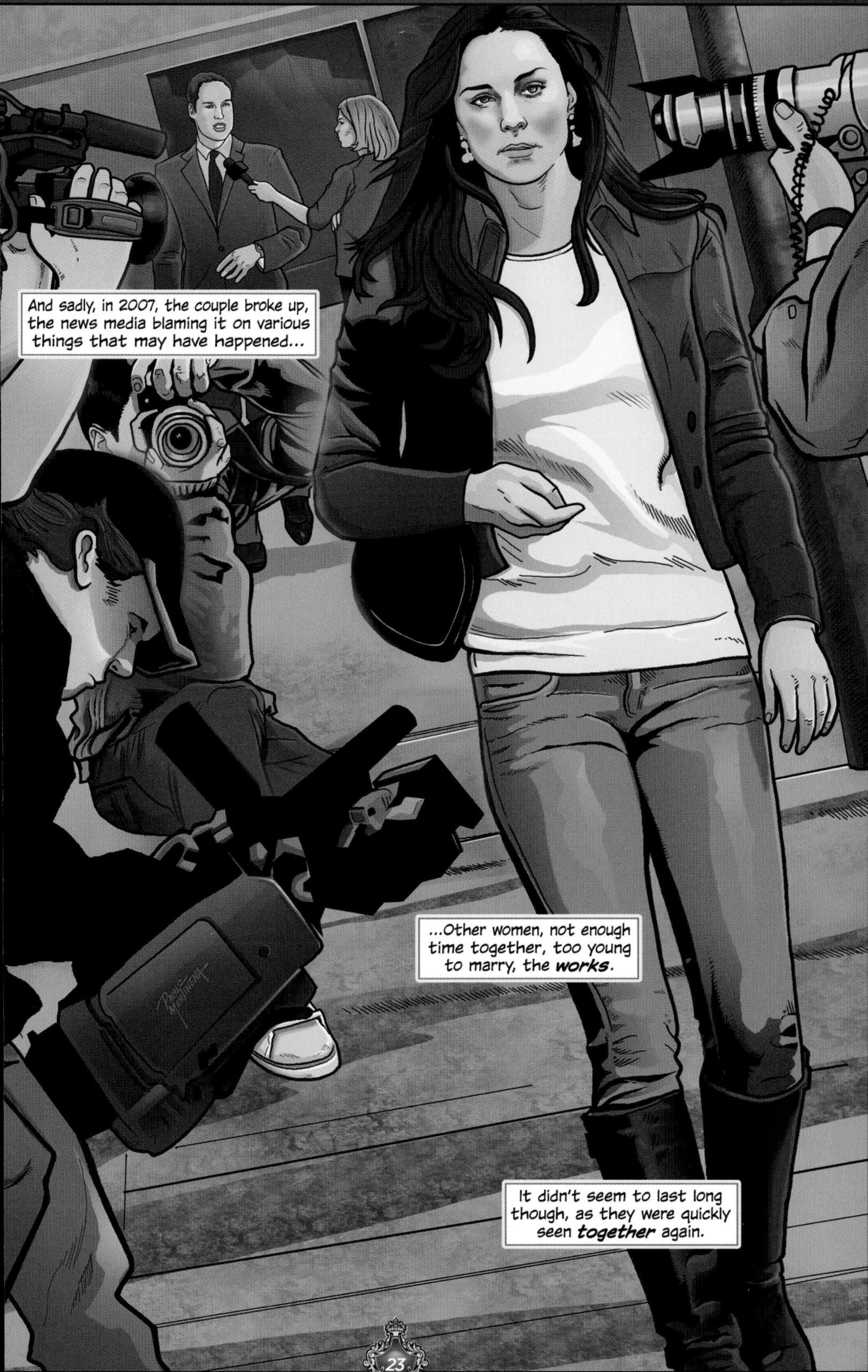
And sadly, in 2007, the couple broke up, the news media blaming it on various things that may have happened...
...Other women, not enough time together, too young to marry, the ***works***.
It didn't seem to last long though, as they were quickly seen ***together*** again.

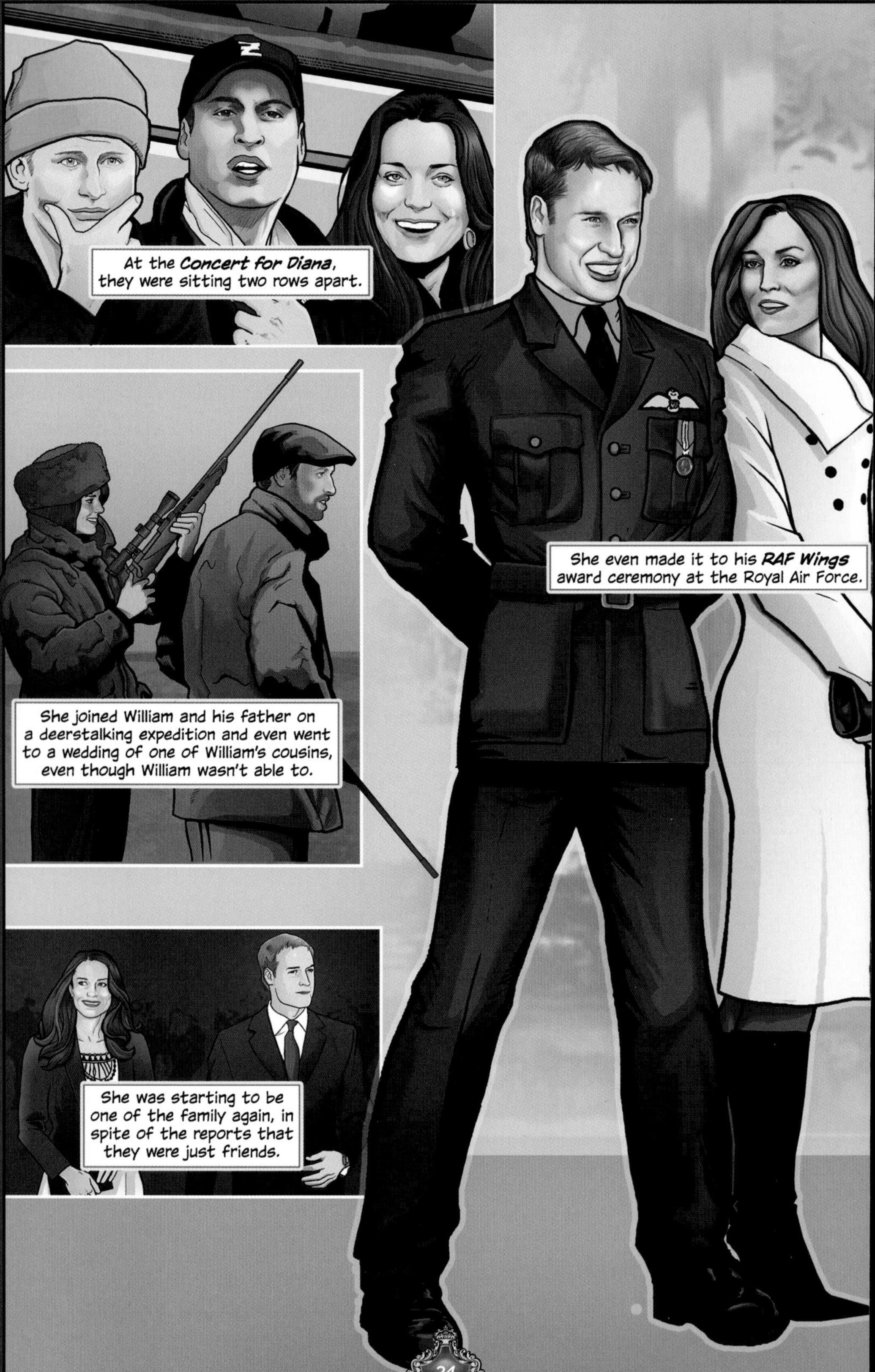
At the Concert for Diana, they were sitting two rows apart.
She joined William and his father on a deerstalking expedition and even went to a wedding of one of William's cousins, even though William wasn't able to.
She was starting to be one of the family again, in spite of the reports that they were just friends.
She even made it to his RAF Wings award ceremony at the Royal Air Force.

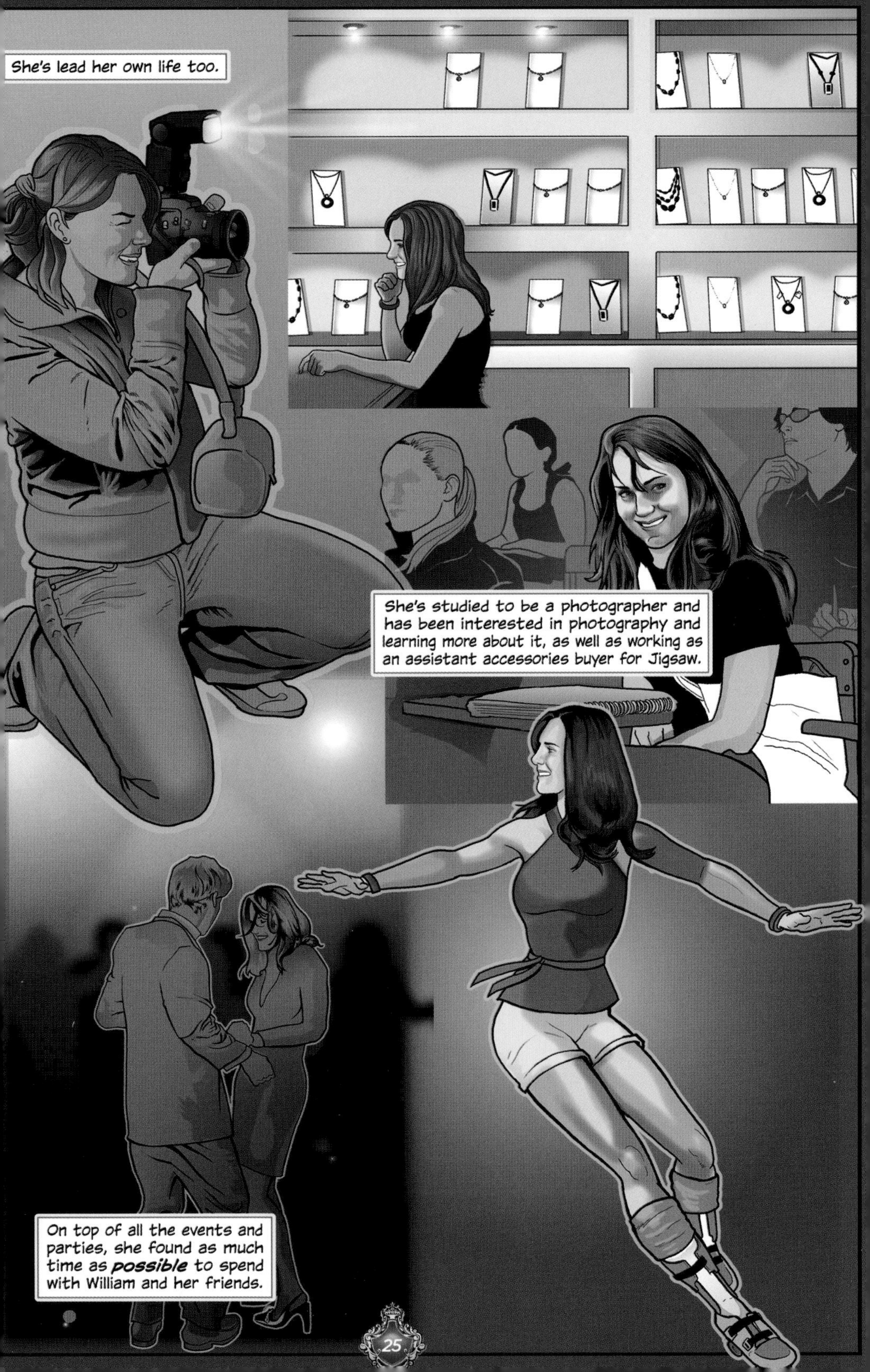
She's lead her own life too.
She's studied to be a photographer and has been interested in photography and learning more about it, as well as working as an assistant accessories buyer for Jigsaw.
On top of all the events and parties, she found as much time as ***possible*** to spend with William and her friends.

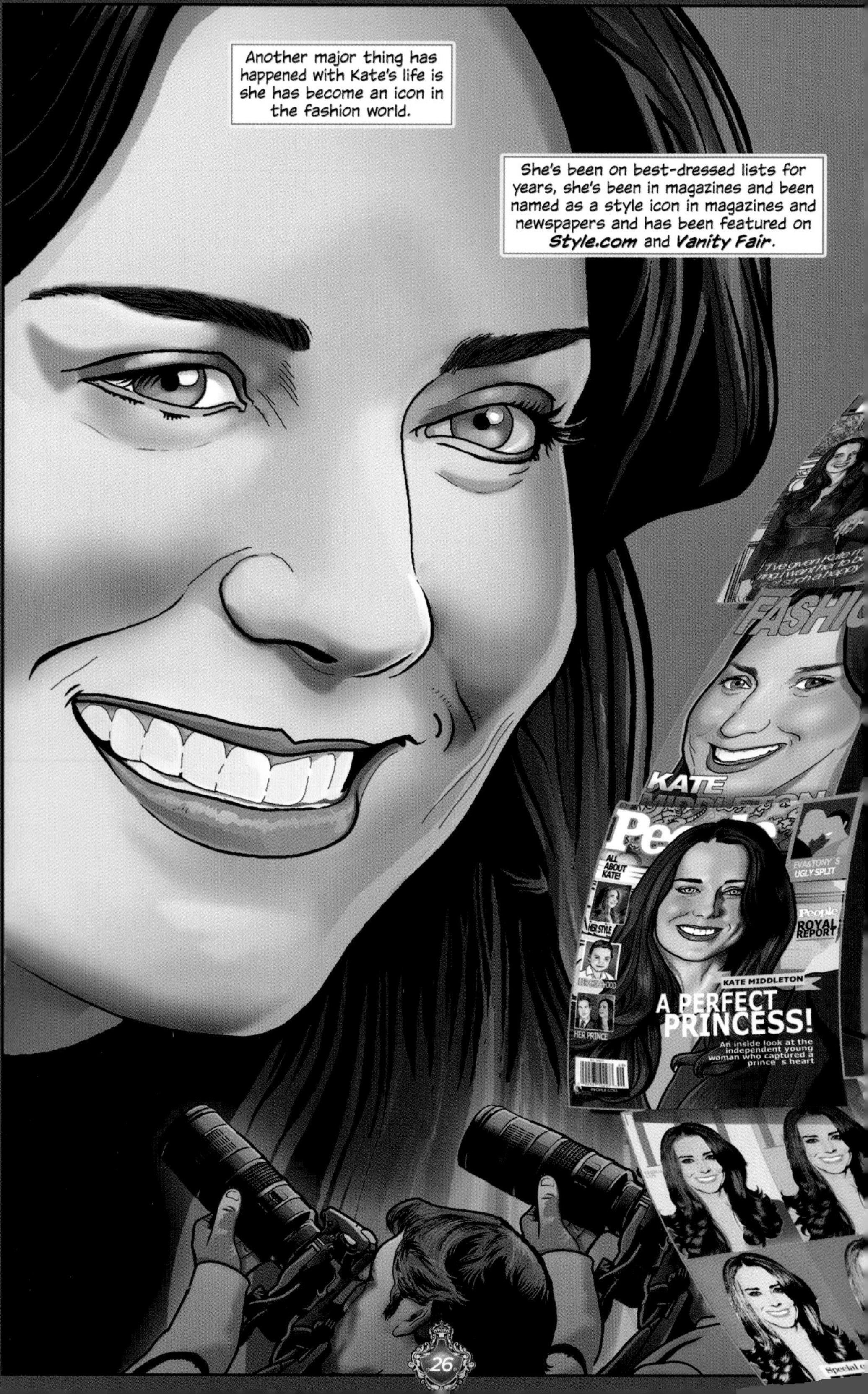
Another major thing has happened with Kate's life is she has become an icon in the fashion world.
She's been on best-dressed lists for years, she's been in magazines and been named as a style icon in magazines and newspapers and has been featured on ***Style.com*** and ***Vanity Fair***.
KATE
ALL ABOUT KATE!
HER STYLE
HER PRINCE
EVA&TONY'S UGLY SPLIT
People
ROYAL REPORT
KATE MIDDLETON
A PERFECT PRINCESS!
An inside look at the independent young woman who captured a prince's heart
PEOPLE.COM

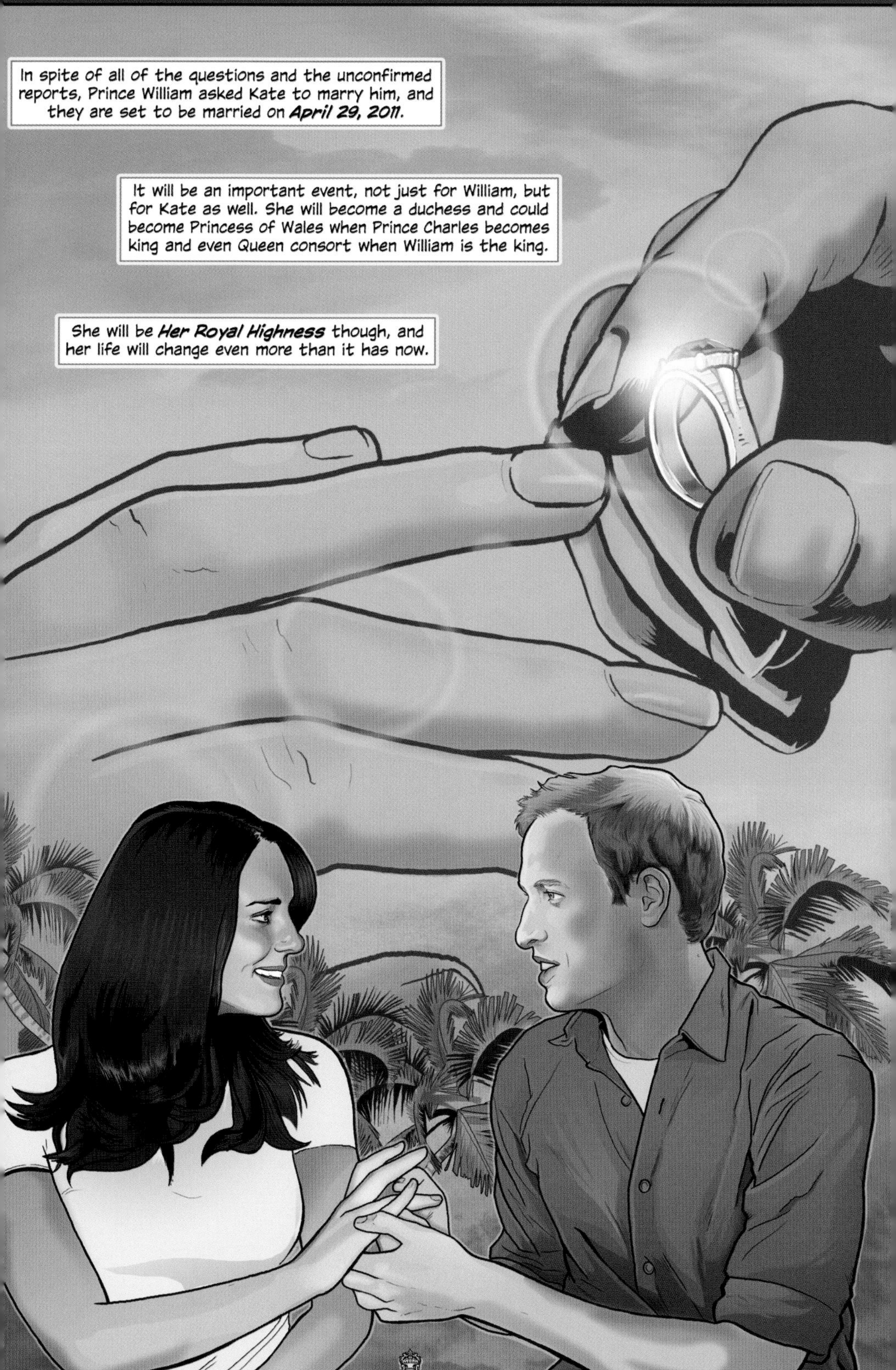
In spite of all of the questions and the unconfirmed reports, Prince William asked Kate to marry him, and they are set to be married on ***April 29, 2011***.
It will be an important event, not just for William, but for Kate as well. She will become a duchess and could become Princess of Wales when Prince Charles becomes king and even Queen consort when William is the king.
She will be ***Her Royal Highness*** though, and her life will change even more than it has now.

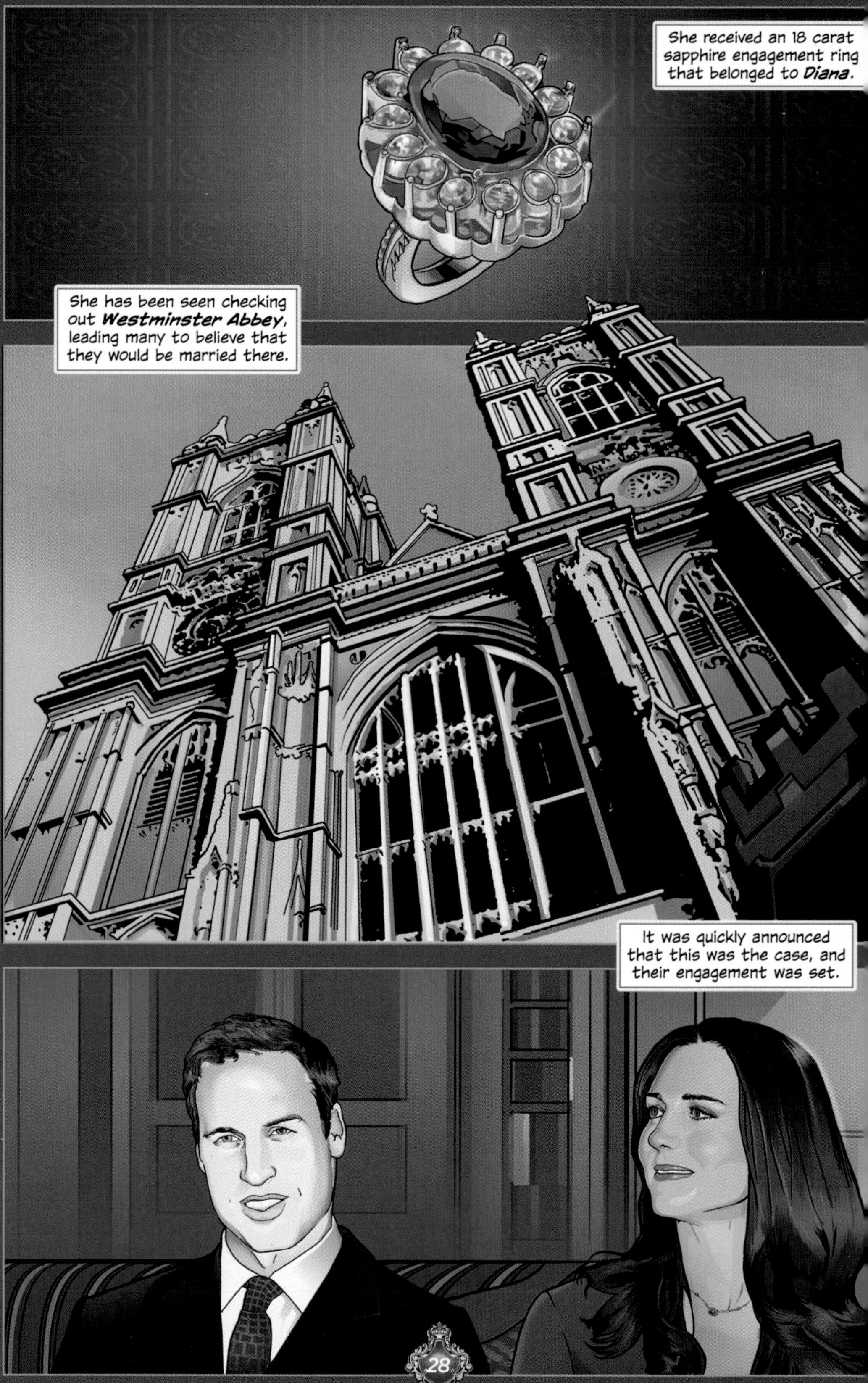
She received an 18 carat sapphire engagement ring that belonged to ***Diana***.
She has been seen checking out ***Westminster Abbey***, leading many to believe that they would be married there.
It was quickly announced that this was the case, and their engagement was set.

Their wedding will be a massive event on a global scale. The media has paid attention to their every move since they began dating, and now with the impending wedding, the attention will *grow*.

Kate Middleton and *Prince William* are to be *married*, and the world will watch as their romance continues to blossom for the rest of their lives.

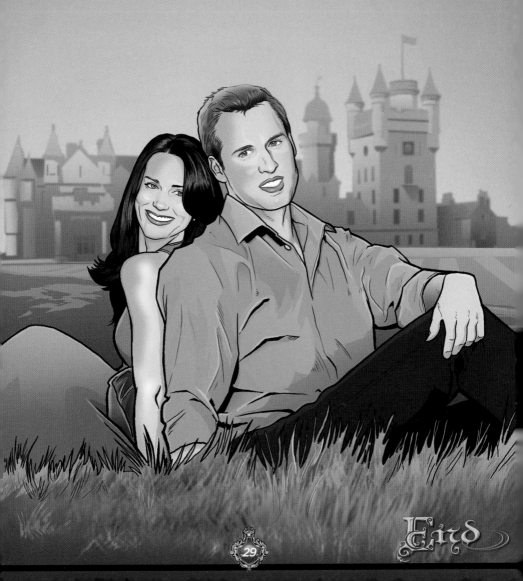

End

BONUS IMAGES

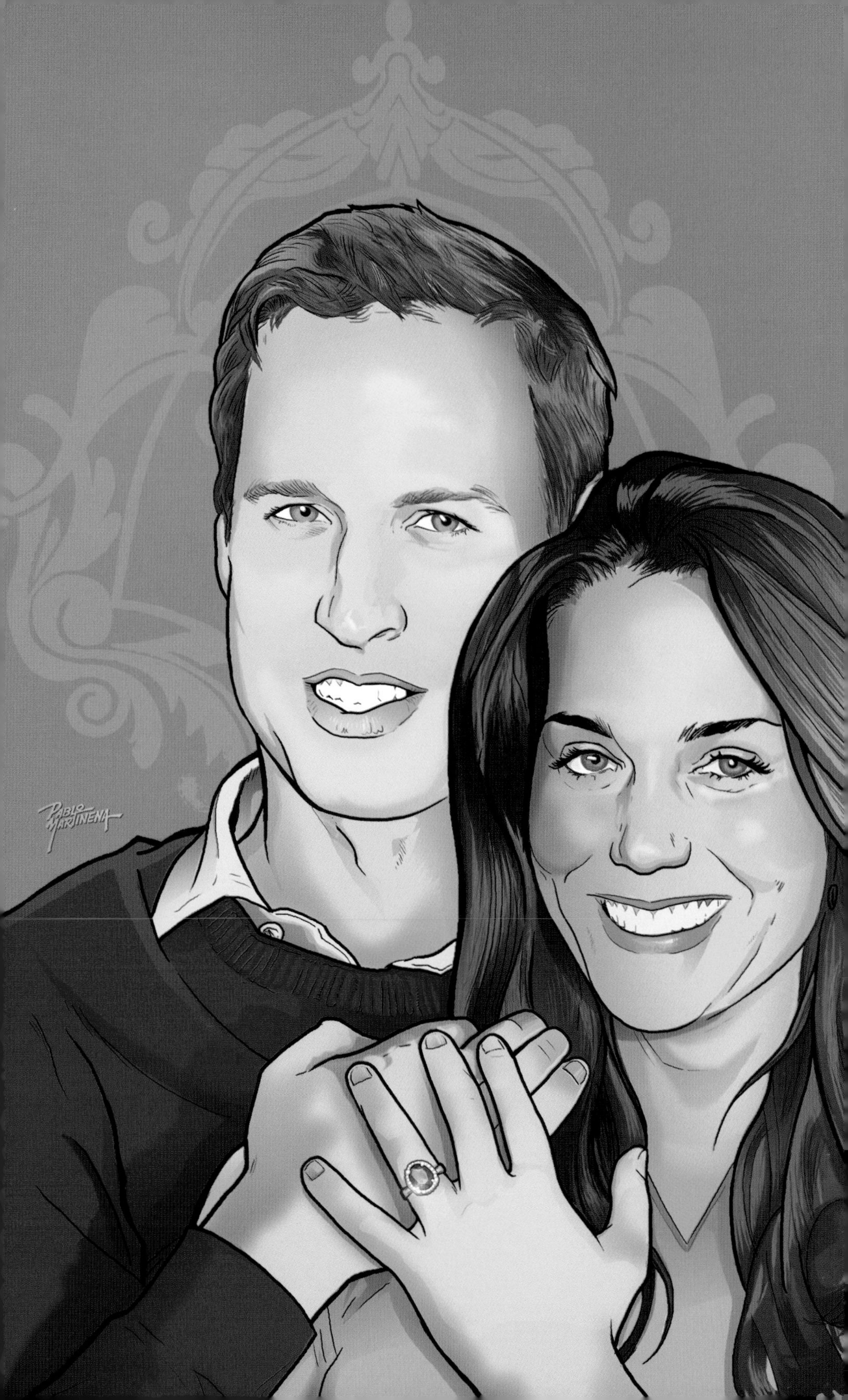
PABLO
MARTINENA

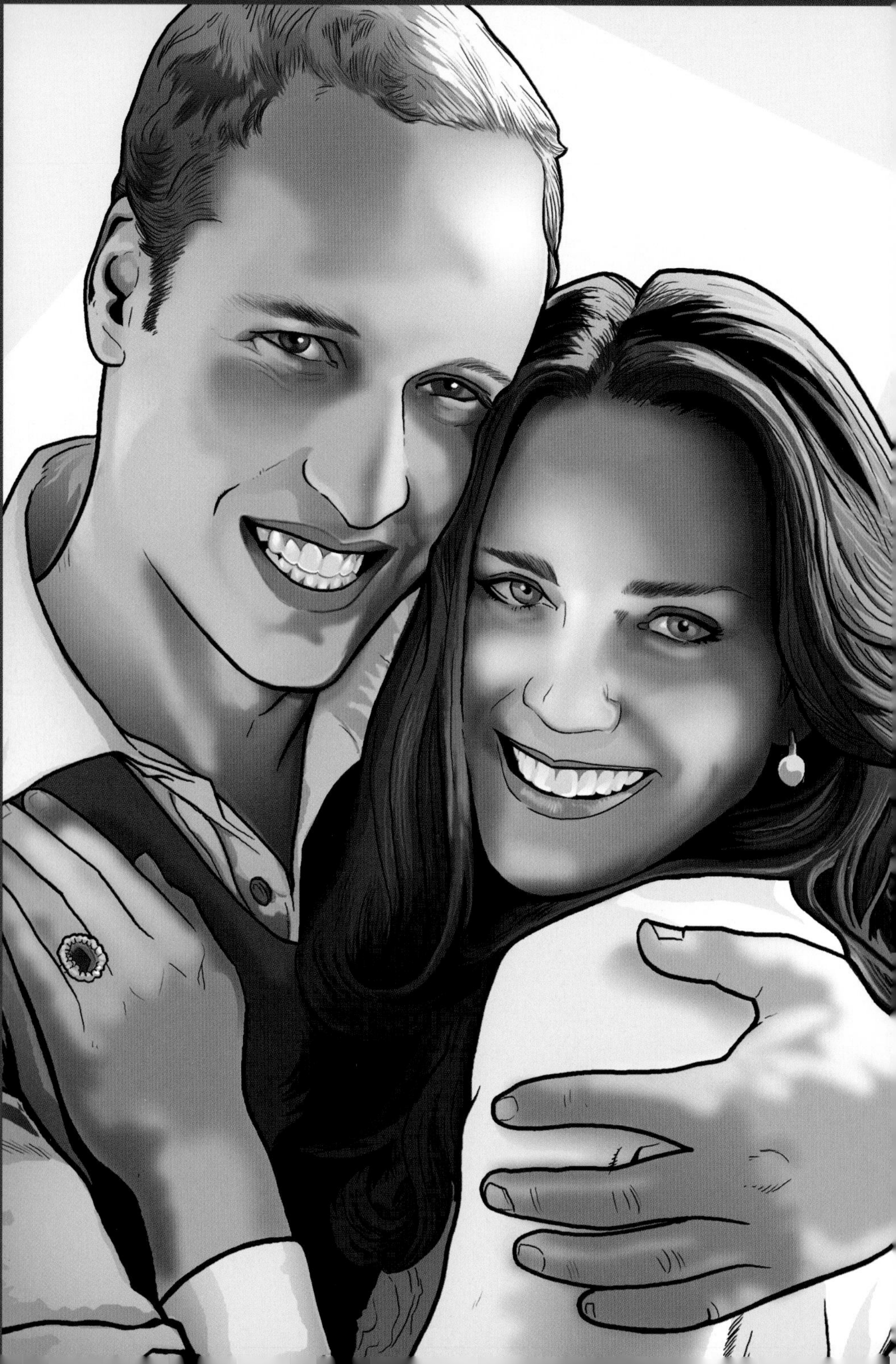

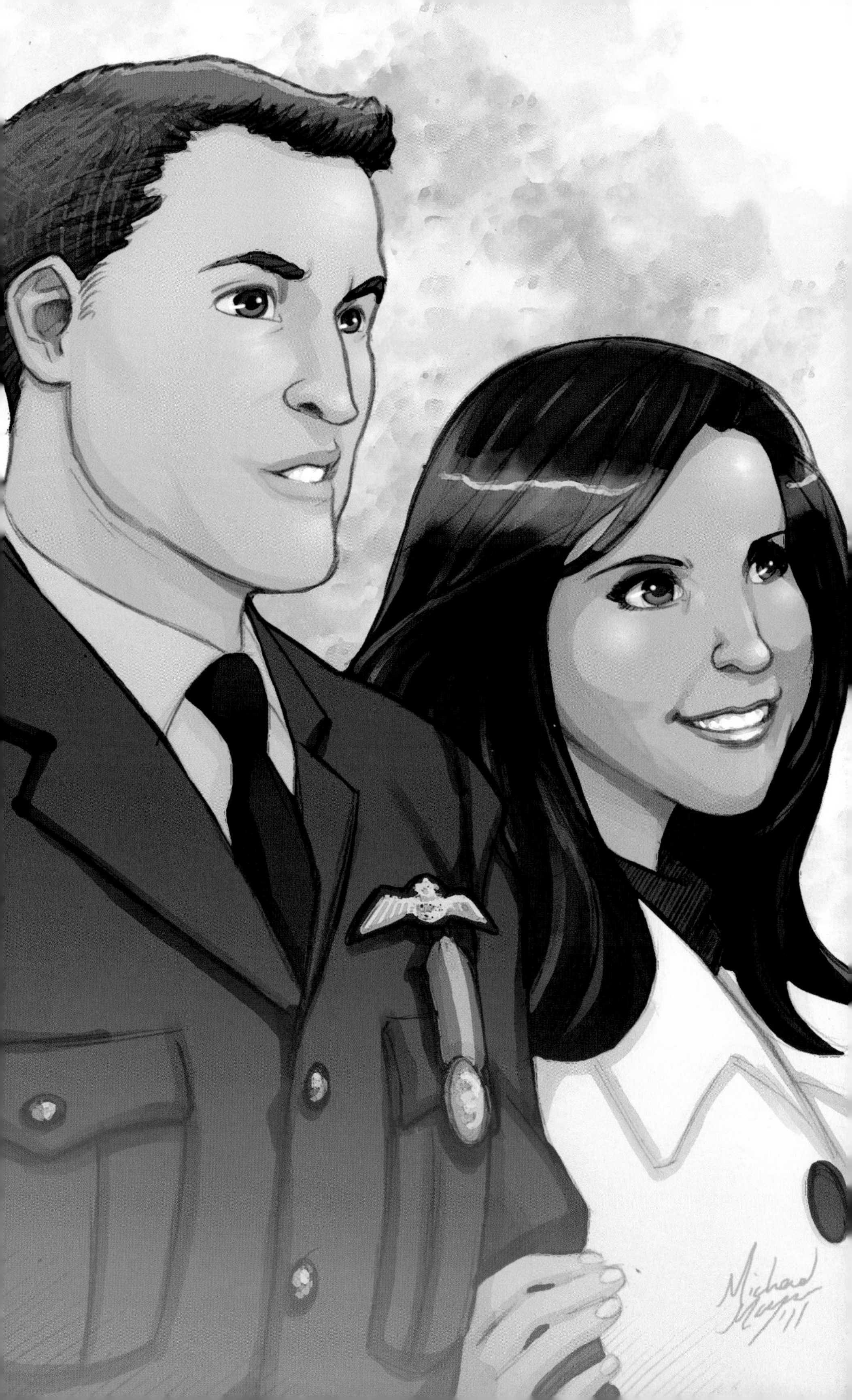

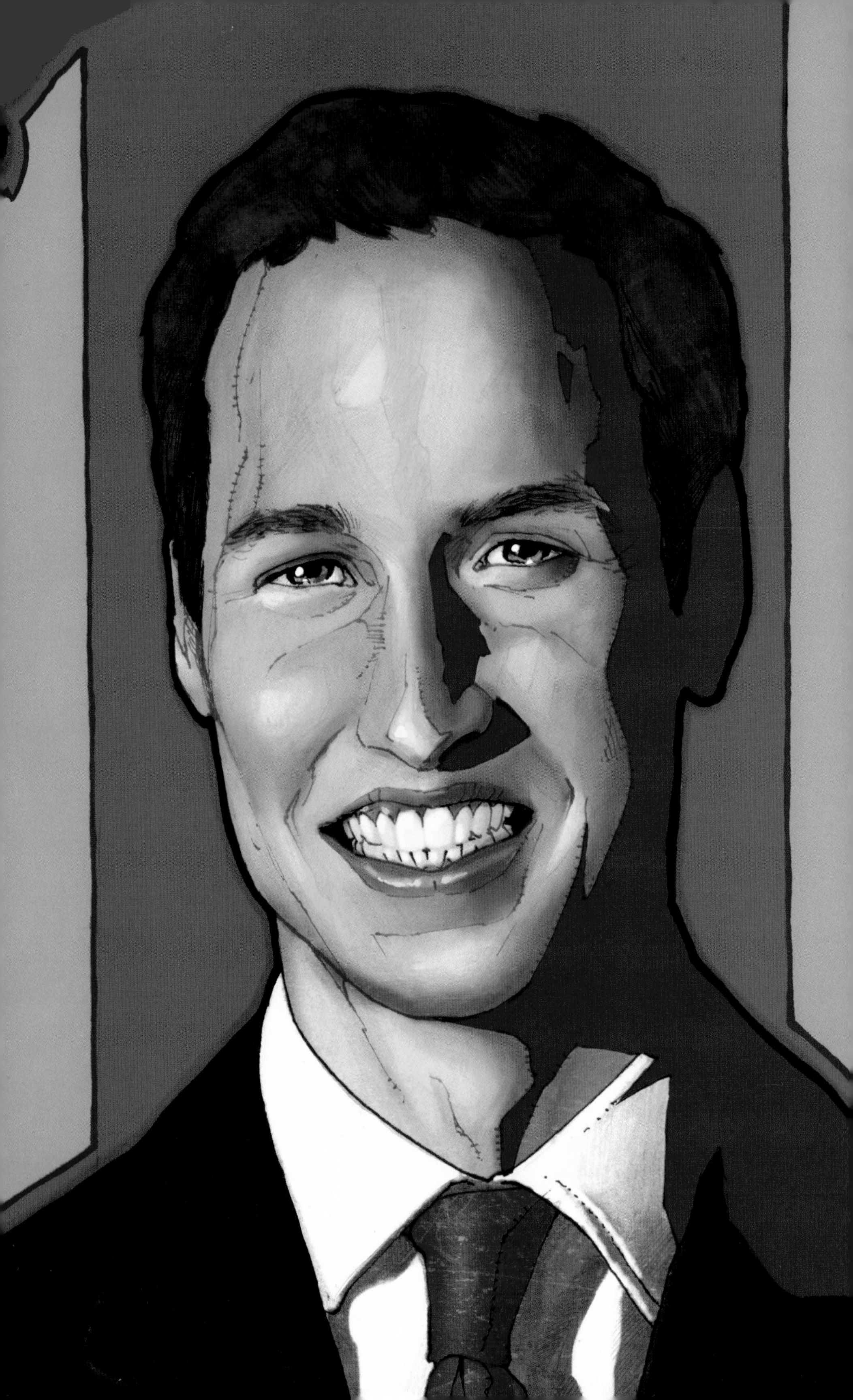

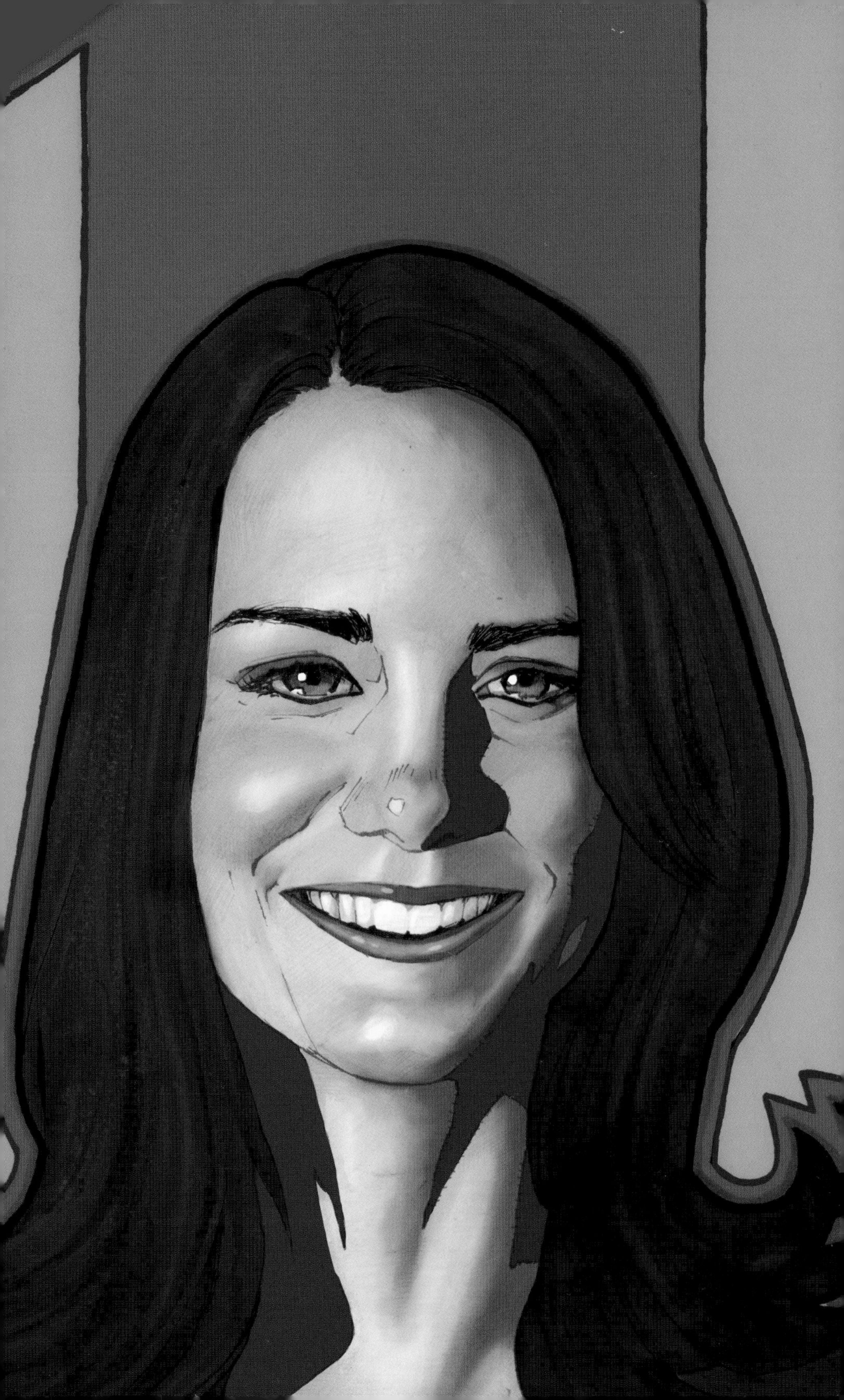

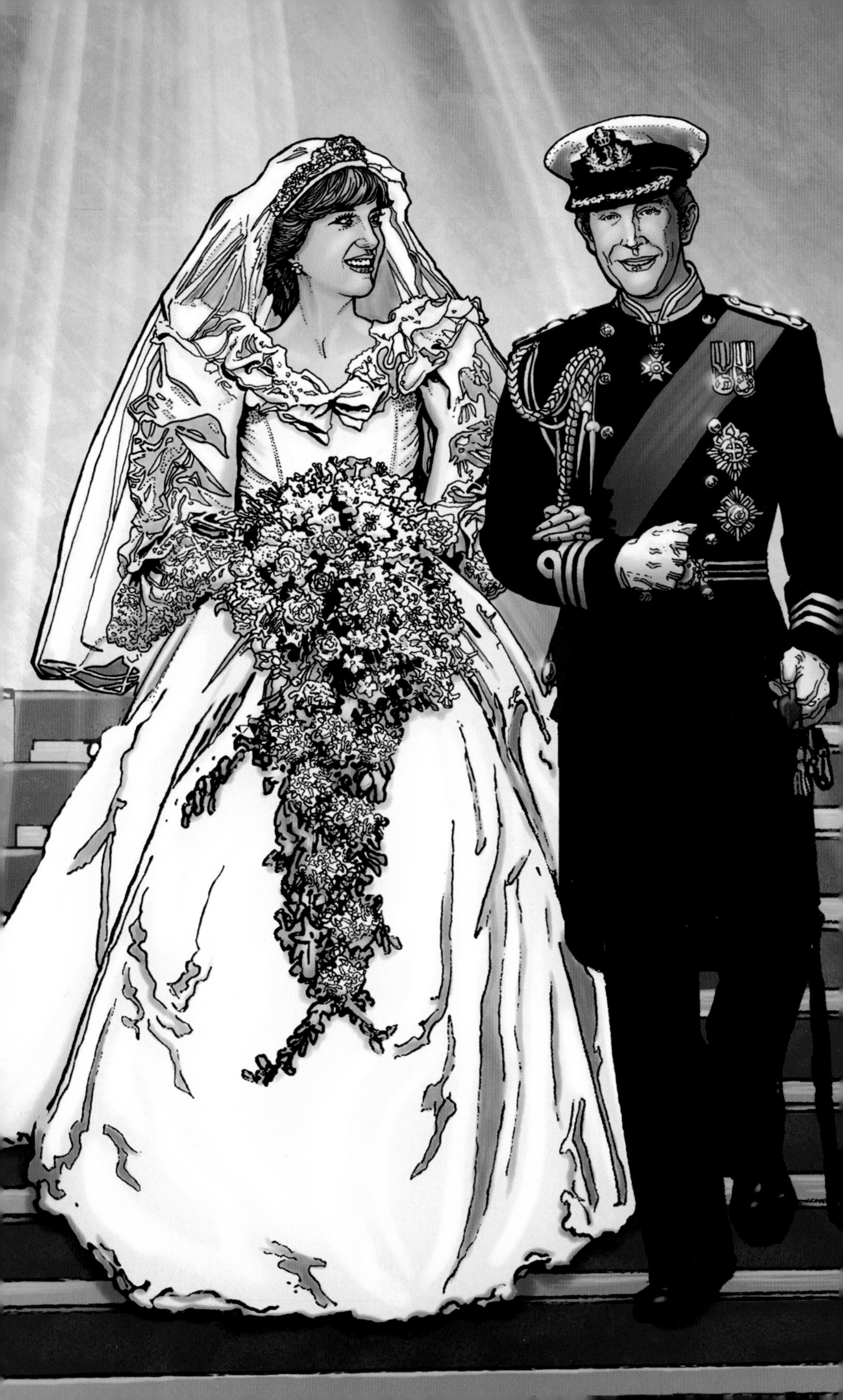

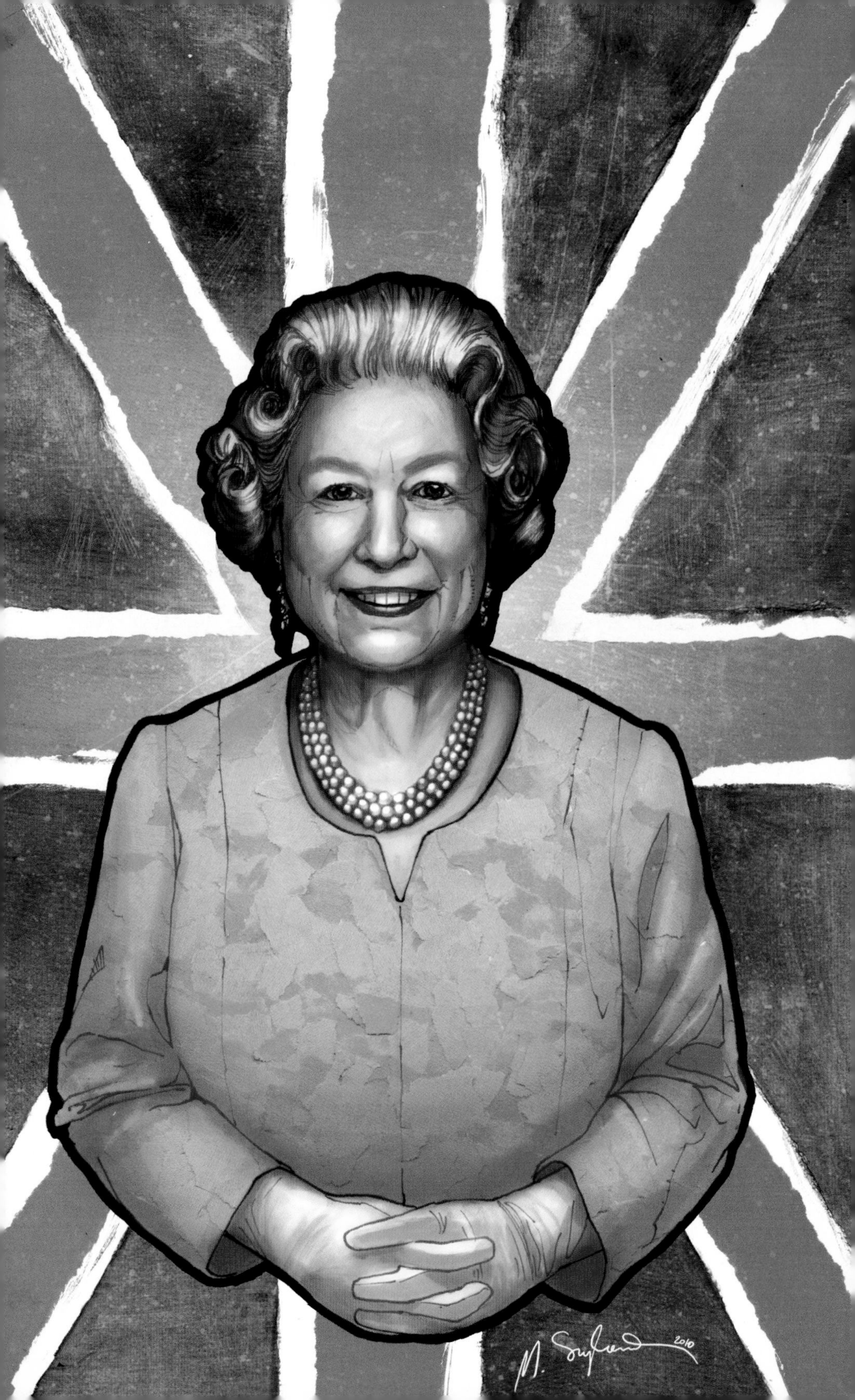
2010

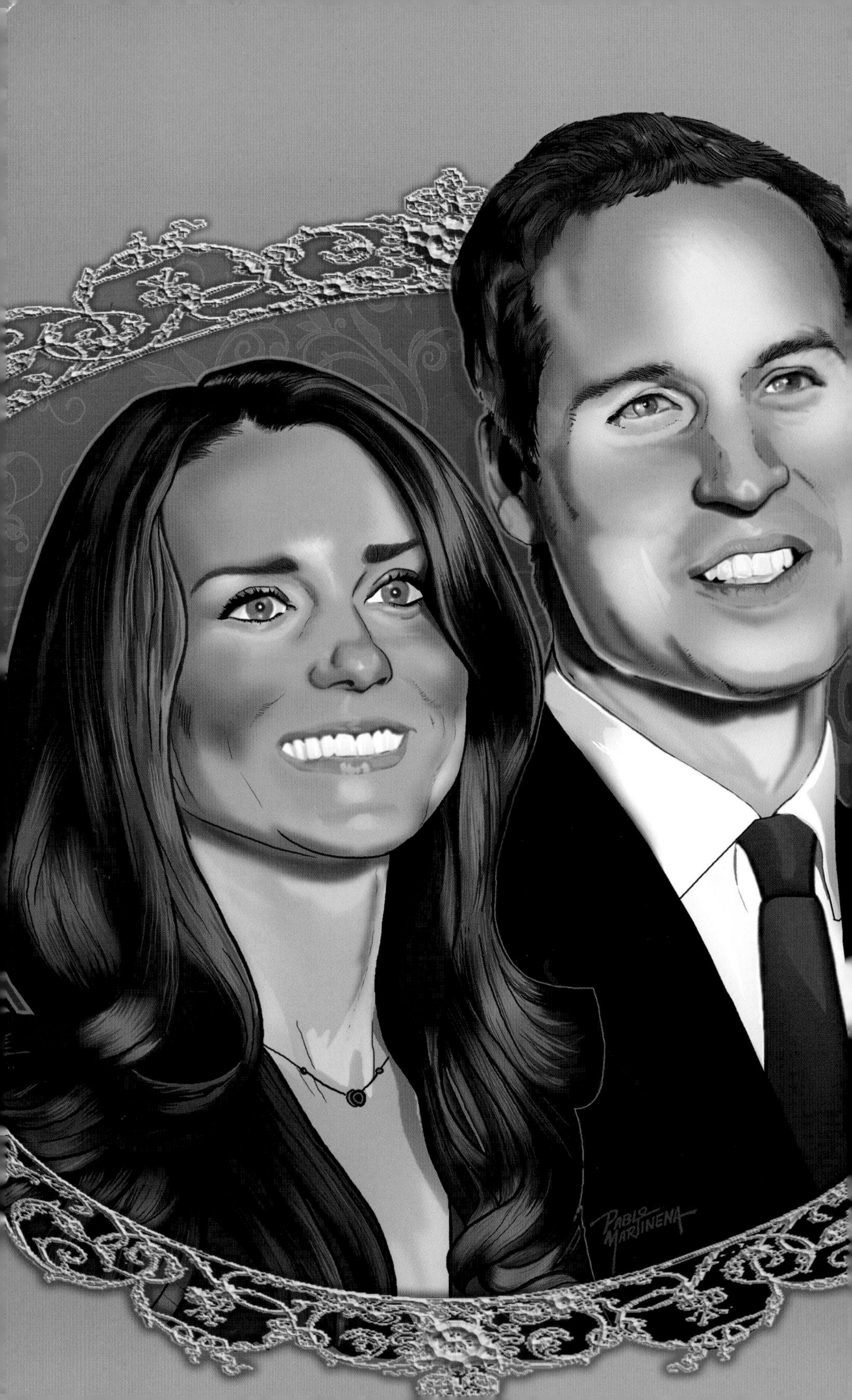
PABLO MARTINENA

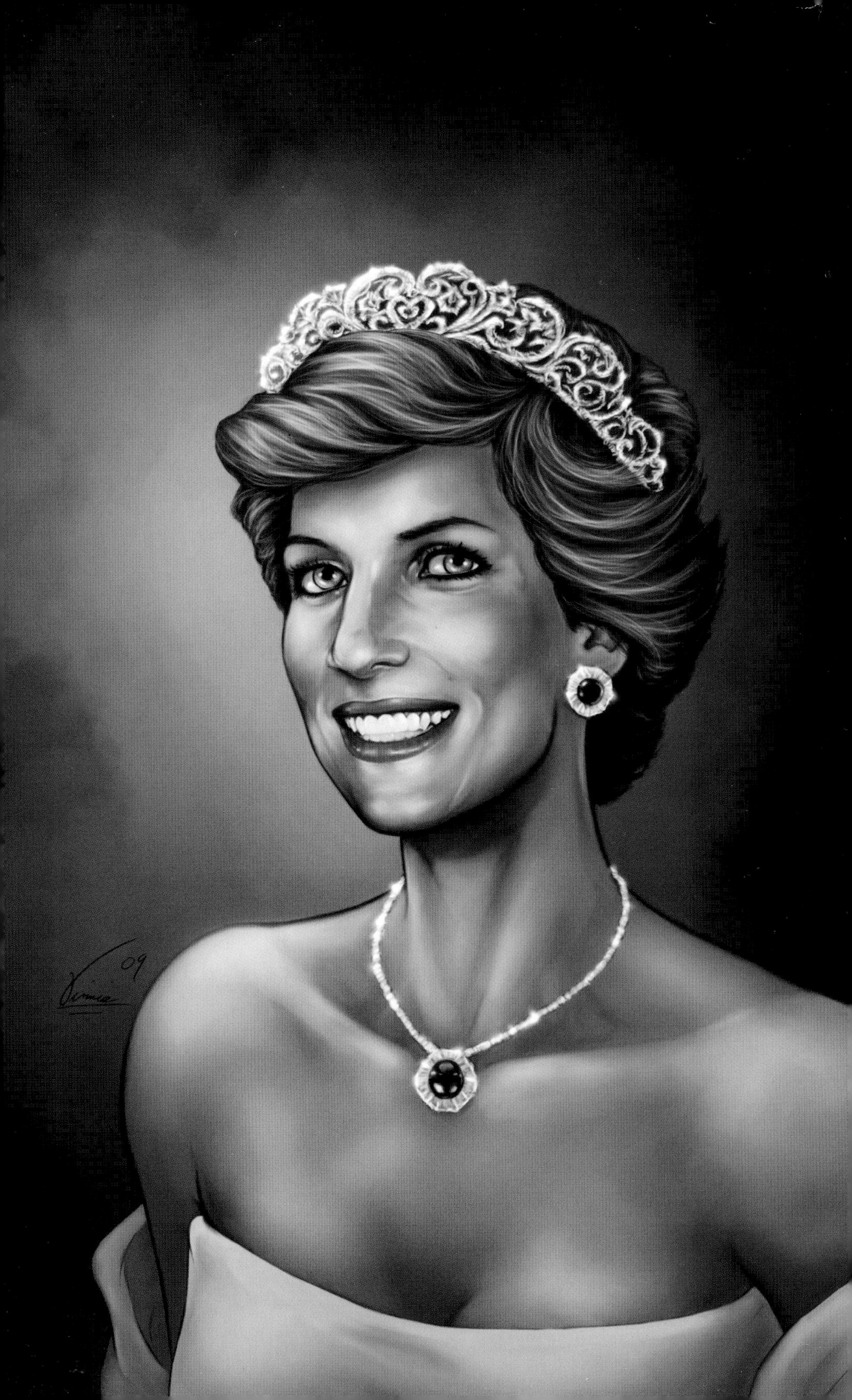

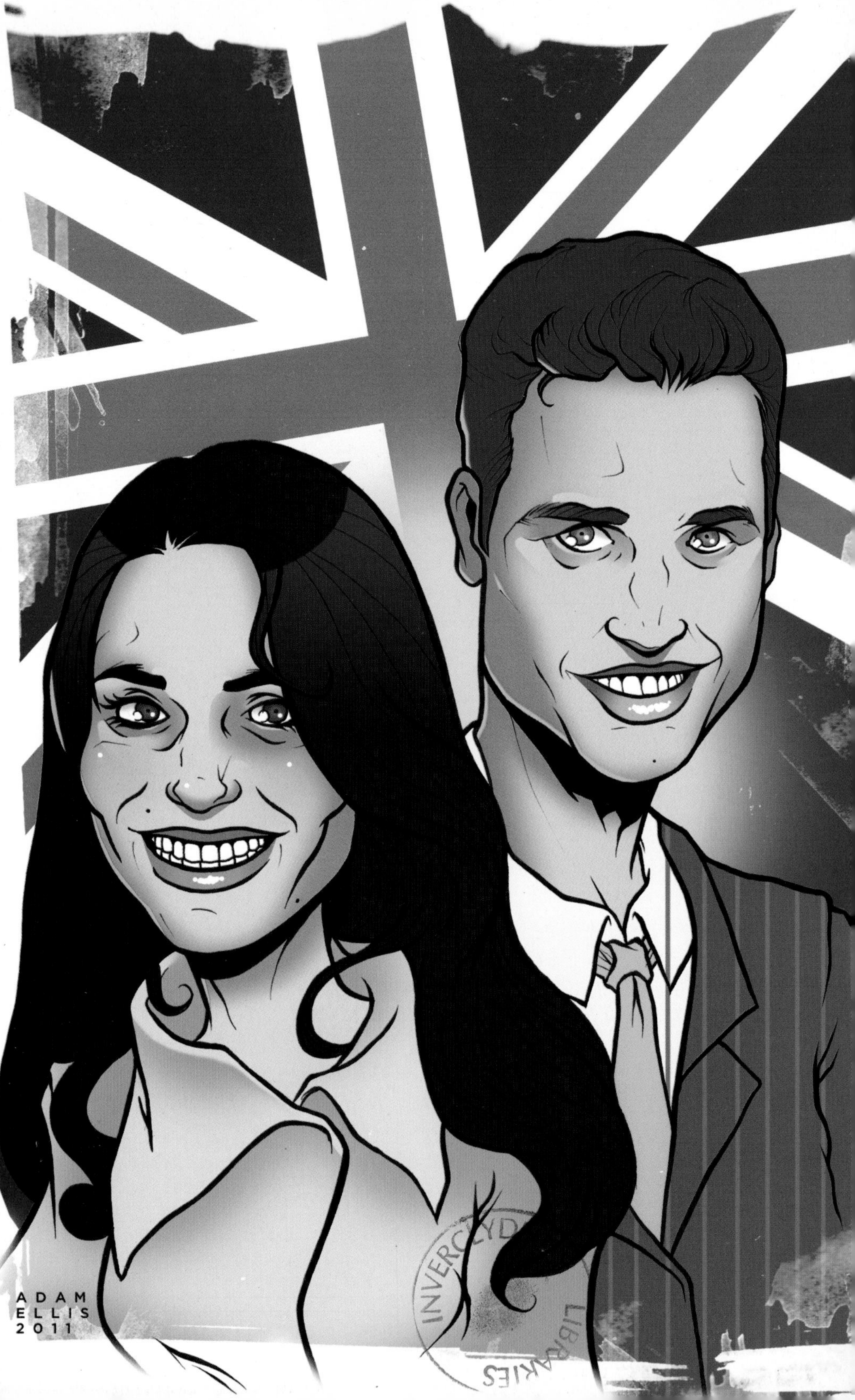
ADAM
ELLIS
2011